AN ENIGMA OF BRONTËS

Novels by Maureen Peters

ELIZABETH THE BELOVED
KATHERYN, THE WANTON QUEEN
MARY, THE INFAMOUS QUEEN
BRIDE FOR KING JAMES
JOAN OF THE LILIES
FLOWER OF THE GREYS
THE ROSE OF HEVER
PRINCESS OF DESIRE
STRUGGLE FOR A CROWN
SHADOW OF A TUDOR
SEVEN FOR ST CRISPIN'S DAY
THE CLOISTERED FLAME
THE WOODVILLE WENCH
THE PEACOCK QUEEN
HENRY VIII AND HIS SIX WIVES
THE MAID OF JUDAH
THE GALLOWS HERD
FLAWED ENCHANTRESS
SO FAIR AND FOUL A QUEEN

AN ENIGMA OF
BRONTËS

MAUREEN PETERS

LONDON
ROBERT HALE & COMPANY

© *Maureen Peters 1974*
First published in Great Britain 1974

ISBN 0 7091 4479 2

Robert Hale & Company
63 Old Brompton Road
London SW7

PRINTED IN GREAT BRITAIN BY
CLARKE, DOBLE & BRENDON LTD.
PLYMOUTH

Contents

Illustrations

ACKNOWLEDGEMENTS

The above illustrations numbered 2, 5, 10 and 11 are reproduced by permission of the National Portrait Gallery. The remaining illustrations were photographed by Walter Scott of Bradford and are reproduced by permission of the Brontë Society.

Acknowledgements

I would like to express my grateful thanks to Mrs Jean Lewens for permission to quote from those Brontë letters of which she owns the copyright, and to the Council of the Brontë Society for allowing me to quote from those manuscripts in the Haworth Parsonage Museum.

My thanks are due also to Mrs Edith M. Weir, for her advice and practical encouragement.

MAUREEN PETERS,
LIVERPOOL

ONE

To Haworth

No writer, or group of writers, has so caught the imagination of the public as that strange, unsociable family who lived more than a hundred years ago in a place even then described as bleak and remote.

So much indeed has been written that one tends to lose sight of the fact that the Brontës were living people who loved and laughed, ate their dinners and grumbled about the cost of living.

The Rev. Patrick Brontë was the father of six children, of whom certainly four, probably five and possibly six, were geniuses. One imagines that the parents of such children must themselves have been remarkable.

Certainly Mr Brontë had an unusual personality. It takes a man of determined character to find his way from an Irish cabin to Cambridge University. One wonders why he, alone of his family, attempted to better himself. Perhaps the nine brothers and sisters who succeeded him never received the opportunity to try their wings.

Patrick, the eldest, may have been the favourite of the family. Of his father is known very little. It is not even certain how he spelled his name. It appears sometimes as Hugh Prunty, and sometimes as Hugh Brunty, while Patrick himself was entered at the University as Branty. Hugh Prunty—or Brunty—did not, apparently, intend his son to follow his own living as a farmer, and the boy was apprenticed, first to a blacksmith, then to a weaver. He must have continued to study, however, for at the age of sixteen he was appointed schoolmaster in his native parish of Emsdale, County Down. There is a tradition that he attempted to found a school of his own, but that the experiment failed through lack of funds. The tradition has the ring of truth, and may explain from where Charlotte's ambition later sprang.

A series of teaching and tutoring posts followed. One suspects that Mr Brontë was a good teacher. Afterwards, he was to inspire in his own children a desire for knowledge, and one of his employers, the Rev. Thomas Tighe, is believed to have encouraged him to try his fortunes in England. Whether it was Mr Tighe who aided him financially, or whether William Wilberforce, one of the minister's friends, granted the young tutor an annual allowance, is not clear.

It is known, however, that in the year 1802, at the age of twenty-five, he became a student of St John's College, Cambridge. Apart from any allowances granted to him by patrons, he may have received a small grant from the University authorities, and it was possible for an undergraduate to earn modest fees by extra-curricular teaching and coaching.

In 1806, Patrick was ordained as a minister of the established Church of England. Henceforth, he was to spell his name as Brontë. The word is a Greek one—meaning 'thunder'—and as Patrick was a Greek scholar, it is probable that the translation stirred his imagination. Lord Nelson had been created Duke of Brontë in 1799 and this also may have influenced the young Irishman's choice.

Why he decided to change his name has never been determined. Perhaps he wished to emphasize the break between himself and his old life. Although he is said to have sent his mother twenty pounds a year until her death, he never set foot in his native land again.

His first curacy was at Wethersfield, in Essex, where he came very near to marrying his landlady's niece. It is not known precisely why he jilted her. Perhaps her attractions did not outweigh her poverty. In any event, the affair caused Mary Burder to feel lasting resentment, and Mr Brontë appears to have left Essex under a cloud. A brief curacy in Shropshire was followed by a curacy in Dewsbury, Yorkshire. In 1811, he was appointed to a living at Hartshead, just outside Bradford.

The familiar photograph of the Rev. Patrick Brontë is an intimidating one. The erect, white-haired old gentleman in the ridiculously stiff cravat glares sternly over the tops of his rimless spectacles. The nose is high-bridged and haughty, the mouth tightly compressed.*

It requires an effort of the imagination to see him as Miss Branwell must have seen him when she visited her cousins, the Fennels, in 1812. He was then thirty-five years of age, and in the prime of manhood. He was described as strikingly handsome, with a head of red hair and a beguiling Irish brogue. He had high principles, energy and ambition; he was interested in politics and military matters. Well-versed in the classics, his honesty and integrity were beyond question.

He was strongly drawn towards literature. During his curacy at Hartshead, he attempted to supplement his income by writing. He published, at his own expense, two volumes of verse, and two prose tales.[1] Mr Brontë toiled long and hard at his work undeterred by the fact that he possessed not a scrap of talent. He eventually gave up his writing, not because he doubted his own powers, but because writing books did not bring any financial rewards.

Mr Brontë met his future wife less than a year after his arrival at Hartshead and the attraction between them seems to have been mutual from the beginning.

Maria Branwell was the daughter of the lately deceased Thomas Branwell, merchant, of Penzance. She had been reared as a Methodist, but became a member of her husband's congregation. She was six years younger than Mr Brontë, and lived, modestly, on an annual income of fifty pounds.

Although not in the least pretty or elegant, she must have possessed a certain charm, for Mr Brontë completely forgot his own intention to marry for money and proposed to the neat, dainty little Cornishwoman.

Both were past their first youth and both were independent, so, after a brief engagement, the marriage took place. It was actually a double ceremony, because Mr Brontë's friend, the Rev. Morgan, married Miss Jane Fennel at the same time.

* See illustrations.

The marriage appears to have been happy, although much of this may have been due to Mrs Brontë's sweet temper. She had evidently been carefully, if narrowly, educated and before her marriage had tried her hand at literary composition in a tract entitled *The Advantages of Poverty in Religious Concerns*. After marriage she was plunged at once into a succession of pregnancies. Maria was born in 1814, a year after the marriage, followed in about twelve months' time by Elizabeth. Mrs Brontë was pregnant for the third time when she and her husband moved to Thornton, where the most famous members of the family were born. Charlotte arrived on 21st April 1816; Patrick Branwell on 26th June 1817; Emily Jane on 30th July 1818; Anne on 17th January 1820. The youngest was scarcely three months old when the Brontës left Thornton, and moved to Haworth, where Mr Brontë accepted the perpetual curacy.

The circumstances of his appointment are interesting. Mr Brontë had been offered the living in 1819, but, hearing that the Church Trustees had not been consulted, wisely resigned. Accordingly, a certain Samuel Redhead became incumbent of Haworth. His appointment was extremely unpopular, and the villagers quickly showed their disapproval by dragging the unfortunate minister from his pulpit and rolling him in a bag of soot. Not unnaturally, Mr Redhead resigned, and the living was again offered to Mr Brontë, who, having ascertained that it met with general approval, agreed.[2]

Haworth is high in the West Riding of Yorkshire, some four miles from Keighley, the nearest market town. There is nothing intrinsically romantic or beautiful about this commonplace village. Granted that it is lonely and was lonelier still in the Brontës' day, when a hired gig served as transport for the entire population, yet its houses are packed tightly together like gossiping old women, and long before its associations brought flocks of tourists, the place must have hummed with activity as the women bustled about their housework while the children played marbles on the well-whitened doorsteps.

The people of Yorkshire are noted for their blunt speech, money sense and lack of sentiment. In Haworth, these characteristics were particularly pronounced. Although they despised idle curiosity, many housewives must have lingered behind their curtains on that cold February day, as seven carts lumbered up the steep and twisting main street. Six of the carts were piled with furniture and linen. In the seventh were the members of the new parson's household.

The Parsonage stands above the rest of the village and is hidden from view by the Parish Church. Today, a new church stands on the site of the one where the Brontës worshipped, and an extra wing, housing a museum, has been built on to the back of the house. But the house itself is the same grey stone Georgian dwelling where the Brontës were to spend the greater part of their lives.

In front of the house is a strip of garden, hidden from the lane which divides it from the back of the church by a high brick wall. The lane runs along the side of the house towards the moors. On the other two sides, the Parsonage is surrounded by the graveyard. Many of the headstones lean drunkenly against the outer walls, and from every window one can see tombstones, until one imagines that the dead are trying to strangle the living.

The Brontë children took little interest in the graves. Their eyes were fixed upon the prospect of the moors beyond. From the beginning, the moors drew them like a magnet, and they spent every available moment exploring the unbounded countryside.

Even today, the hills around Haworth have a wild, forbidding aspect. Snow lies thickly on them during the winter, and the driving wind twists the trees and bushes into fantastic shapes at all seasons of the year. But one may still find great bunches of heather and gorse in the long valley grass, and tickle trout in the bubbling streams as Emily once liked to do.

They had ample opportunities in which to discover the hidden beauties of their environment. Mrs Brontë, already ailing when they left Thornton, survived the move for barely more than a year. Her death was due to an internal cancer, but it has been suspected that the disease was aggravated by consumption.

Mr Brontë, with the manifold duties of an unfamiliar parish by day, and the care of a dying wife by night, had no time to spare for the six small children. His wife's elder sister, Miss Elizabeth Branwell, had come with the family to help them settle into their new home. She remained to take care of her sister, and must have been only too thankful to be able to bustle the little ones out of doors, with Nancy or Sarah Garrs to chaperone them.

Villagers remembered them in after years—undersized, shabby children with "wild eyes".

Locked in her sick room upstairs, Mrs Brontë must have sometimes heard their treble voices, raised in triumph as they clambered over the stile. She seldom expressed any desire to see them, so that Charlotte retained only a faint memory of her mother being carried downstairs after tea to play with Branwell.[3]

The Parsonage itself was, and remained, an austere place. The rooms were much smaller than one would have imagined after seeing the exterior of the building. Four rooms open off the square, arched hallway. Mr Brontë used one of the front apartments as his study. Behind this was the kitchen, which led into a back kitchen, or scullery. On the left of the hall was the family sitting-room, which served also as dining-room and parlour. Behind the sitting-room was a smaller room where stores were kept.

Upstairs were four bedrooms opening off a square hall. Mr and Mrs Brontë used one bedroom, and the favoured only son had the slightly larger chamber beyond. Another room was turned into a bed-sitting-room for Aunt Branwell, and the servants squeezed into the room next door. There was also a smaller room at that time, scarcely more than a closet, where some of the children probably slept.

In the centre of the semi-circle is the most famous place in the house. Scarcely more than a lobby, with no fireplace, and a window directly above the front door, it was called the children's study, and given to them as their own. Every night, trestle beds were put up in it for Maria and Elizabeth to sleep upon.

The Brontës were not wealthy, and the Parsonage lacked any touch of luxury. One of Mr Brontë's obsessions was an abnormal dread of fire. He believed, quite rightly, that cotton and flannel, being inflammable, were very dangerous to wear. So his children were clad in wool or silk. Fire was, indeed, in that era of long skirts, a real danger, but Mr Brontë carried his theory to extremes. He would allow no curtains to be hung at the windows, nor any carpets, except in the sitting-room and study. Elsewhere there were bare flagstones underfoot.

Despite bare windows and floors, the place was not entirely comfortless. Peat was burned all the year round, and there were red sofas and armchairs to strike a note of gaiety. In the study, the narrow bookshelves were crammed with literature, and flowers or grasses were arranged in vases.

When Mrs Brontë died in 1821, her eldest child was only seven years old; thus the mother was never to know anything of the sublime talents of her children.

NOTES TO CHAPTER ONE

1. The Rev. Patrick Brontë, *Cottage Poems*, *The Rural Minstrel*, *The Cottage in the Wood* (story) and *The Maid of Killarney* (story).
2. Record of Incumbents of Haworth Parish Church.
3. Daphne du Maurier, *The Infernal World of Branwell Brontë*.

TWO

Cowan Bridge

Of the two eldest girls, Maria especially exerted a considerable influence over the younger members of the family.

No portraits exist of them. They were described to Mrs Gaskell as small and delicate in appearance, but no further details are known, although Charlotte, describing Maria in the guise of Helen Burns, wrote of her gentle, pensive expression.

Something of Maria's intellect is known, but even there the knowledge is second hand, for not a scrap of her writing has been preserved. Mr Brontë declared that she was the cleverest of his children and his assertions were borne out by other witnesses. They remembered how five-year-old Maria used to accompany her father to the local publishing offices at Thornton, and there, seated on a high stool, correct the proofs of Mr Brontë's manuscripts. Mr Brontë recalled also how it was Maria's custom to read the newspaper every day and then to discuss political events as sensibly as an adult. She was then all of seven years of age.

After her mother's death, Maria tried to take Mrs Brontë's place as guide and comforter to the younger ones. The housekeeping was undertaken by Miss Elizabeth Branwell, Mr Brontë's sister-in-law. Already in her forties, she was a small, tightly-corseted lady, with chestnut hair. Her gowns were a trifle too young for her, and her mob-caps very large. She wore wooden pattens on her feet to protect them from the cold flagstones, and took snuff from a little gold box.

It must have been hard for a spinster, already set in her ways, to leave a comfortable home in the green south and spend the rest of her life in a neighbourhood she detested in order to care for children who were not even her own. As a strict Methodist, Aunt Branwell knew where her duty lay, but she appears to have derived neither pleasure nor contentment from the doing of it.

It was Maria who taught Charlotte and Branwell how to read and count, and who escorted them to church and helped them over the stile on to the moors. And it was Maria who took Branwell into her bed when he awoke sobbing from a nightmare.

An interesting question arises. Did Maria also invent for the other children a secret world into which they could all escape? It is generally assumed that Branwell first thought of the imaginary land where they could play out their deepest desires. Could it not have been Maria who first cheered them with stories of the strange and brilliant landscape where fantasy became reality?[1]

Mr Brontë, in a letter to Mrs Gaskell, wrote: "When mere children, as soon as they could read and write, Charlotte and her brother and sisters used to invent and act little plays of their own in which the Duke of Wellington, my daughter Charlotte's hero, was sure to come off conqueror."

It was natural that the father should mention by name the one daughter who had tasted the fruits of success, but in the very next paragraph he seems to indicate clearly that Maria and Elizabeth were still alive when the little plays were acted.

It was Maria who told the others of what she had read in the newspapers. From her, Charlotte must have heard, and been fascinated by, exploits of the gallant Duke. It is very probable that Maria directed their plays, even if Charlotte did like her favoured hero to win all the battles. If she did invent the secret world, her original conception of it must have been very different from what it later became.

Maria was seven years old when her mother died—old enough to understand her loss and yet not old enough, surely, to bear it with quite the high stoicism with which she has been credited.

Maria must have thought of her mother as being in Heaven, and described it to the others until they too saw clearly the tall, shining towers. It is significant too, that Charlotte, writing of the establishment of their plays, should begin with an apparently irrelevant mention of a geography book which Mr Brontë had once lent to Maria. The bright, coloured maps, with the vast expanses of sea between, may have stirred the girl's lively imagination.

Branwell and Charlotte certainly originated the "great plays", but Charlotte says explicitly that these were not the "secret" plays. Perhaps when the children invented their cloud land, they were merely remembering the ways in which that gentle, elder sister had once sought to amuse them.

Eventually, the children had to go to school. Branwell was entered as a pupil at Keighley Grammar School, but there is no evidence he ever attended that establishment.[2] Perhaps the travelling involved was too great for a small boy, or perhaps he had already begun to show traces of the epilepsy that was to crucify him in later life.

Mr Brontë, devoted to his only son, may have decided to keep the boy at home where a quiet, regular life might mitigate the fury of the nervous spells. So Branwell, deprived of competition with other children, studied alone, and his father, having no basis for comparison, readily believed in his genius.

The little girls were sent away to school. It was necessary for them to receive an education because, one day, they must earn their own living. Maria and Elizabeth were sent to a school in Wakefield, but were removed within a short space of time.[3] Presumably, Mr Brontë had been informed of a new school for the daughters of clergymen recently established at Cowan Bridge.[4]

Their entry was delayed when the whole family went down with measles and whooping cough. They were barely convalescent when their father, in the hired gig, escorted them the twenty-odd miles to the school. Maria was eleven years old. Elizabeth was ten.

The Rev. Carus Wilson had founded the school for the

daughters of clergymen in reduced circumstances, and Mr
Brontë had gone to inspect the premises before sending his own
daughters there. He was apparently satisfied with the long, low
buildings, situated amid very pretty countryside, and the lack
of carpets and curtains eliminating any risk of fire.

Maria and Elizabeth entered the school in July 1824, and
eight-year-old Charlotte joined them a month later. In November of that same year, Emily was also sent to her sisters.[5]

In this day and age, it is almost impossible to arrive at an
accurate conclusion about the school. It must be judged, not
by our standards, but by the standards of the nineteenth century. Children were then looked upon not as privileged beings,
but as little savages who must be moulded, forcibly if necessary,
into responsible, God-fearing adults. Hell was no theological
concept but a very real place with which disobedient children
were constantly threatened. Corporal punishment was usually
acted upon, even by the most loving parents.

Privations were held to be good for the soul and there were
many privations at Cowan Bridge. The children wore plain,
grey dresses and had their hair cropped to discourage vanity.
They slept in long, narrow, unheated dormitories and ate food
so badly cooked as to be almost inedible. All her life Charlotte
remembered, with loathing, the burnt oatmeal, the stews with
lumps of rancid fat and the sour rice pudding.

At many a meal both children and staff went hungry, but
complaints to Mr Wilson were ignored. The pupils must be
taught to despise material needs, and the mistresses were told
to stick to their appointed task of teaching. Ill-paid and largely
unqualified, the mistresses appear to have fallen into two cate-
gories. There were those who did everything in their power
to make the children comfortable, and those who vented their
own frustrations upon the unfortunate pupils.

Maria, and to a lesser extent, Elizabeth, appear to have
suffered greatly from the harsh discipline. Maria's precocity
was ignored, her lack of skill with a needle and her untidiness
and daydreaming were constantly punished, while her gentleness, far from awakening pity, seems to have aroused some
members of the staff to conduct which falls little short of
sadism.[6]

Incredibly, none of the girls complained of their treatment.

Complaints would, in any event, have met with little response. The children were, at least, receiving an education, and Maria probably impressed upon her younger sisters the need for silent endurance.

In the spring of 1825, a "low fever" broke out at Cowan Bridge. The disease was probably typhus, spread by overcrowding and primitive sanitation. The pupils, weakened by lack of exercise and poor food, sickened rapidly. Oddly, none of the Brontës caught the fever, although while it ran its course, lessons were suspended and the school became a sick-bay. Perhaps the staff were too occupied with the typhus victims to notice the seriousness of Maria's condition. When it became evident that she was, indeed, gravely ill, her father was requested to take her home.

Maria died on 6th May 1825,[7] shortly before her twelfth birthday, displaying, according to Mr Brontë, "many symptoms of a heart under Divine influence". She was buried beside her mother beneath the aisle of the church, and a month later, Elizabeth lay beside them.[8] Ten-year-old Elizabeth, of whose intellect and character nothing is known, died also from consumption, but in her case the disease appears to have remained unsuspected until a few days before her death.

As Charlotte and Emily were at home when their second sister died, the effect upon them was even greater than if they had been away at school. Mr Brontë grieved for the loss of his eldest children. Charlotte and Branwell grieved for the loss of one who had been a mother.

For the rest of her life, Charlotte was to attempt to fill Maria's place. And for the rest of her life, she was to dread that the symptoms of consumption might appear in other members of the family. Every cough, every cold, was anxiously commented upon in her numerous letters, every change in the weather carefully noted. One senses that her solicitude was not always appreciated—that the others resented her constant fussing. But Charlotte had watched Maria dying slowly under the indifferent or hostile eyes of the teachers.

To the child of nine, both sisters became martyrs—and the remaining three doubly precious.

NOTES TO CHAPTER TWO

1. Charlotte Brontë, *History of the Year 1829*.
2. Local tradition states this, but no record of his name exists in the registers.
3. The school was run by Miss Richmal Crompton whose book *Questions* held a high place in every Victorian schoolroom.
4. Copy of prospectus of Cowan Bridge in Howarth Parsonage Museum.
5. Journal of Education, 1900.
6. Charlotte Brontë, *Jane Eyre*.
7. Death Certificate of Maria Brontë.
8. Death Certificate of Elizabeth Brontë.

THREE

The Infernal World

For five years the Brontës remained in Haworth, with an occasional visit to Thornton to see Anne's godmother, Miss Frith—this their only contact with the world beyond. The Parsonage was, in many ways, like a greenhouse, in which unseasonable flowers may be forced to bloom before their time.

Mr Brontë taught Branwell himself, instructing him in Latin and Greek, and for some reason, instructing Anne in Latin.[1] Aunt Branwell gave a simpler form of instruction to the girls, but there is no evidence of its being inferior. The strict little Cornishwoman was well read, and wrote a literate hand. Mr Brontë possessed a considerable number of books, and no censorship was imposed upon their reading matter.

The children were familiar with the classics of Homer, Virgil, Milton, and Shakespeare. They owned copies of novels by Scott and Fielding, as well as some volumes of poetry by Wordsworth, Cowper, and Coleridge. In addition, they were not debarred from reading Lord Byron's *Don Juan*, or the Gothic romances of Maria Edgeworth.[2] Books which did not appear on the Parsonage shelves were borrowed from the Mechanics' Institute Library, at Keighley, and from the Heaton family at Ponden Hall.

Both Mr Brontë and Aunt Branwell subscribed to various newspapers and periodicals. *Leeds Intelligencer, John Bull*, and

Blackwood's Magazine were eagerly perused and discussed by the whole family. Aunt Branwell lent them copies of *Lady's Magazine* and *Methodist Magazine*.

Children were expected to learn certain accomplishments, so it was no surprise to hear that the Brontës received music lessons once a week from the church organist, and later, the services of a drawing master, Mr William Robinson of Leeds, were engaged.

Branwell was allowed to play with other boys from the village, provided that they were Sunday School members. The girls were expected to perform certain household tasks, and to sew or knit.

Mr Brontë encouraged his children to keep pets, and a succession of dogs, cats and birds passed through the Parsonage. This was resented by Aunt Branwell, who disliked animals and forbade the dogs to come beyond the kitchen,[3] but the girls continued to care passionately for all dumb creatures.

After tea, which the whole family ate together, the children were free to ramble about on the moors during the long, light evenings, or to play up in the little study where Maria and Elizabeth had once slept. The four children possessed few toys, but needed few. Even before Maria's death, they had acted playlets in which the leading political figures of the day played important roles. Now these plays were to be elaborated—to assume an importance that cannot be exaggerated.

All imaginative children play out dream fantasies. The spectacle of a child who has been punished for naughtiness venting anger upon a doll or other inanimate object is familiar. Familiar too, is the shy, only child who invents an imaginary companion, often blamed by the child for the child's misdeeds. But few children can have invented their own dream worlds with such intensity, or dwelt in them for so long.

The Brontës were never conscious of having been unhappy as children. Indeed, they harked back to that period as a time of innocence and joy. Yet there is something basically unhealthy in the eagerness with which they escaped into what Charlotte called "the infernal world", or the "place beneath".

This infernal world had its conscious origin in some toys that Mr Brontë brought back as gifts after a visit to Leeds. The girls were apparently uninterested in the ninepins, the toy village and the dancing doll, but fell eagerly upon the box of wooden soldiers intended for Branwell.

Emily and I jumped out of bed, and I snatched up one and exclaimed: "This is the Duke of Wellington. This shall be the Duke." When I had said this, Emily likewise took up one and said it should be hers; when Anne came down, she said one should be hers. Mine was the prettiest of the whole, and the tallest, and the most perfect in every part. Emily's was a grave-looking fellow, and we called him "Gravey". Anne's was a queer little thing, much like herself, and we called him "Waiting Boy". Branwell chose his, and called him "Buonaparte".[4]

The little wooden soldiers have vanished long ago, broken or discarded. But from the foregoing account, it is evident that the little figures were of varying shapes and sizes. All of them were to be christened eventually, by such names as Ross, Parry, and Sneaky. The soldiers were tangible objects over which the children could exercise complete control. They could be made to perform incredible feats of daring, made to bear the sins of their owners, and to possess some of those owners' characteristics.

The "Twelves" or "Our Fellows" were amalgamated with the game of "The Islanders". Each child had, on some previous occasion, chosen an Island and peopled it with their favourite characters. Charlotte had chosen the Isle of Wight, Branwell the Isle of Man, Emily the Isle of Arran, and Anne Guernsey. These were known as "best plays".

Our plays were established; "Young Men", June, 1826; "Our Fellows", July, 1827; "Islanders", December, 1827. These are our three great plays, that are not kept secret. Emily's, and my best plays, were established 1st December, 1827; the others March, 1825. Best plays mean secret plays; they are very nice ones. All our plays are very strange ones. Their nature I need not write on paper, for I think I shall always remember them.[5]

The "great plays" were not, at first, kept secret. The adults were well aware that the children were, in Tabby's phrase, "always scribbling", but writing kept the children quiet, and Mr Brontë, valuing privacy himself, never intruded upon the privacy of others.[6]

The "African Adventure", was a fusion of the "Twelves"

and "The Islanders". Branwell is credited with its invention, but the geography book in which the relevant maps were found must have been pointed out to him by Maria long before.

The children wrote down their stories on small pieces of paper, stitched down the middle to form booklets. Some of the tiny magazines are less than two inches square; others larger with illustrated wrappings. The prose and poetry within is written in a tiny script which resembles print and requires a magnifying glass to read.[7]

Originally begun as the chronicles of the wooden soldiers, the books were probably scaled down in proportion to the little figures. Later, as the "infernal world" tightened its grip, the minute script was a shield against the prying, and possibly disapproving, eyes of the adults.

The "Twelves" land after a stormy voyage, upon the coast of New Guinea. The desert, according to Charlotte, is a place of desolation, once the scene of battles between good and evil genii. The Young Men conquer the Ashantee who occupy the desert and build a city with the help of four genii, called Chief Genius Tallii, Chief Genius Brannii, Chief Genius Emmii, and Chief Genius Annii. The realm is called Verdopolis, with its capital of Glass Town, and the Duke of Wellington its elected ruler.[8]

At some point, Emily and Anne broke away and formed a kingdom of their own, called Gondal,[9] with its neighbouring province of Gaaldine. The Glass Town confederacy continued, with the scope of the story being widened and more and more characters being introduced.

Wellington's two sons became the Duke of Zamorna and Lord Charles—the elder being dark, passionate and satanic; the younger an embodiment of moral virtue. Charlotte wrote constantly of the tempestuous Zamorna, with his numerous illicit affairs. Zamorna, with his passions, illegitimate children and fiery temper, is a Byronic figure. Charlotte married him first to the gentle Marian Hume, and then to Mary Percy, daughter of the Earl of Northangerland.

As Charlotte's hero was Zamorna, so Branwell identified himself with Northangerland. Originally, introduced as Alexander Rogue, he was described by Charlotte as "rather polished and gentlemanly, but his mind is deceitful, bloody and cruel".[10]

Rogue, executed in one episode, was resurrected by Branwell and given the title by which he was later known. Branwell gave Northangerland three wives and at least two mistresses, by whom he had various children. One of these, Mary Percy, who married Zamorna, became Branwell's favourite heroine.

It was in 1834 that Charlotte and Branwell, having exhausted the possibilities of Verdopolis, moved their characters eastward to the territory of Angria.[11] Henceforth, Angria was to be the "infernal world". Branwell, in childhood had described, with boyish gusto, the various battles, rebellions and counter revolutions of the place beneath. As he grew to manhood, he concentrated more and more upon Northangerland, "Lucifer, Star of the Morning". Hitherto, he had written in the first person. Now, he re-told episodes in his hero's life from the point of view of one of his discarded mistresses, Harriet O'Connor.

It is significant that Branwell, although picturing himself as Northangerland, could submerge himself so convincingly in a feminine personality.

Harriet's older sister, Caroline, dies and thus Branwell, reliving his childhood tragedy, could write again of his own dead sister, pouring out his grief and horror as the coffin lid was closed.[12]

Branwell's contribution to Angria was immense, despite the absurd melodrama of much of his verse. Northangerland *was* Branwell, with his faults magnified, his dreams translated into action, devoid of the conscience which tormented the boy. The story, as Branwell matured, became increasingly one of lost faith and desolate despair. Northangerland, military hero and faithless lover, was Satan's own child. So did Branwell see himself, forgetting that he was just the parson's son, but allowing himself the luxury of grief in the cynicism of his hero.

Charlotte's own creation, Zamorna, was Northangerland's bitterest enemy. Yet the two men have the same qualities of passion and ruthlessness. But, in Zamorna's case, the constant threat of damnation, the religious doubts, are lacking.

Adolescence is a difficult, transitional period. Charlotte, with her vigilant conscience forever crushing her dawning sexuality, could play out her deepest desires in fictional form. She could gain intense pleasure and relief from her descriptions of Zamorna's involved relationships. Her writing, like Branwell's, is close-packed and often melodramatic, but her descriptive powers are far superior, her characters more subtle, her dialogue more natural.

When she awoke from her "bright darling dream", she was to suffer agonies of remorse for what she considered to be an unspeakable sin. Indeed, her writings are startling in their frankness. In an age when well-bred young ladies fainted at the shock of a proposal, Charlotte's heroines live in sin, content to gratify their passions and to submerge their own identities in the identity of their lover.[18]

For both Charlotte and Branwell, Angria became a drug, and Charlotte fully recognized its dangers.

It is not known precisely how much Emily and Anne contributed to the Angrian Saga. They presumably joined in the secret games, but to what extent is not known.

When Charlotte was sent away again to school, the four children killed off their original creation. They evidently regretted the decision for the writings continued, but while Charlotte and Branwell collaborated closely on their intensely sexual dream experiences, the younger girls began a saga of their own.

The two groups of collaborators wrote of their separate worlds, but appear to have read one another's work, and to have borrowed ideas from one another.

None of the Gondal prose writings have yet come to light, and posterity possesses only a section of the poems. These apparently unconnected, and often undated pieces, are now believed to be the remains of a complete history of Gondal.

The north Pacific island was, like Angria, a place of enchantment. Its early history appears to run parallel to that of Angria, but in other respects it differs greatly. The chief characters were not masculine, but feminine. Gondal is primarily a matriarchy, and its men are destroyed by the love of a woman. This woman is called by many different names—chiefly, Rosina, Alcona, and Augusta. It is not entirely certain if there was only one heroine, or two. Neither is it certain if all Emily's poems fit into the jigsaw puzzle.

The Gondal game was played by Emily and Anne to the end of their lives. Anne, the weaker talent of the two, found, that if things went badly in the real world, it became a tremendous effort to project herself into the dream world. For Emily, the interior dream appears to have continued, not at intervals, but continually.

If Angria is an involved story, Gondal is infinitely more complicated. So many poems were lost, and destroyed, that what remains has to be fitted into some kind of coherent whole.

The Kingdom of Gondal is reft by constant wars between the Houses of Brenzaida and Exina. Julius Brenzaida has a love affair with Rosina of Alcona, and a brief affair with Geraldine Sidonia, who bears an illegitimate daughter. This child, known as Augusta, and sometimes as A.G.A., returns after Geraldine's death to her father's court. According to one interpretation, interest now centres upon this daughter of Julius. A.G.A. proceeds to kill an unwanted child who might block her political career, to marry the child's father who dies in battle, to drive a second lover to suicide, to marry a second time and to seduce the son of this second husband, only to be finally murdered at the instigation of the son's foster sister.[14]

Another interpretation, while following the general outline of the main story, declares Rosina, Augusta, or A.G.A., to have been the same woman. In the second version, Julius is not the father of the heroine but her first great love.

The source of the fantasy worlds were manifold. All the Brontës read newspapers of the day, where the scandals of the Regency were reported with astonishingly little reticence. They were familiar with the legends that abounded in the district of Haworth. Ellen Nussey, Charlotte's friend, later reported that Mr Brontë sometimes told ghost stories to the children. Among them must have been the tale of the apparition of a black dog which appeared to members of the family before death, while at Ponden Hall, the ghosts of Mrs Heaton and her daughter were said to weep in the gardens. Fertile imaginations, and a Celtic leaning towards the supernatural helped. The four children, outwardly obedient and conventional, gathered up every scrap of real or imagined worlds.

It was a world in which they moved freely, released from the inhibitions and frustrations of everyday life. It was a world that was to destroy Branwell. A world from which Charlotte and Anne extricated themselves with difficulty. A world in which Emily's genius was to find the fullest expression.

NOTES TO CHAPTER THREE

1. Copy of *Latin Primer*, annotated by Anne Brontë in Haworth Parsonage Museum.
2. Books in Haworth Parsonage Museum.
3. Letter from Ellen Nussey to Mrs Gaskell.
4. Charlotte Brontë, *History of the Year 1829*.
5. *Ibid.*
6. Letter from Mr Brontë to Mrs Gaskell.
7. Selection of these booklets in Haworth Parsonage Museum.
8. Charlotte Brontë, *A Romantic Tale*, written 15th April 1829.
9. First mention of this occurs in Emily's birthday paper of 1833.
10. Charlotte Brontë, *Characters of Famous Men*, written December 1829.
11. Charlotte Brontë, *Angria and My Angrians*, written in 1834.
12. P. Branwell Brontë, *Poems, circa 1836*.
13. Charlotte Brontë, *Mina Laury*, written 17th January 1838.
14. Emily Brontë, *Gondal's Queen*, arranged by F. E. Ratchford.

FOUR

Portraits

In 1831, Charlotte was sent away to school. She craved knowledge as a flower craves water, but the thought of leaving home again must have been painful. Not only would memories of Cowan Bridge arise to trouble her, but separation from the others meant separation from the "infernal world". At fourteen-and-a-half years of age, Charlotte had yet to learn that she could exist in the place beneath without the presence of her brother and sisters.

Roe Head school was some fifteen miles from Haworth, and Charlotte made the journey there alone, in a covered cart. The school seems to have been a somewhat exclusive establishment. There were seldom more than ten pupils at any one time. The headmistress, Miss Margaret Wooler, ran the school with the assistance of her sisters, and the instruction given was apparently excellent. Italian was taught, as well as French and German and the normal music and drawing lessons reached a high standard.

The building was a gracefully proportioned mansion, set in its own grounds amid rolling hills. The girls were encouraged to take long walks in the surrounding countryside, and to play ball games on the lawn in front of the house.

Miss Wooler was a short, stout person, with braided hair and an air of great dignity. She evidently possessed a kind heart and a quick mind, for her pupils were happy under her direction and spoke highly of her.[1]

Those who watched Charlotte alight at the school gates saw, what Mary Taylor later described as "a little old woman, so short-sighted that she always appeared to be seeking something, and moving her head from side to side to catch a sight of it. She was very shy and nervous, and spoke with a strong Irish accent".[2]

Charlotte spent most of that first day crying into the window curtains and was discovered there by another pupil, Ellen Nussey, who saw her as "anything but pretty. Her naturally beautiful hair of soft, silky brown being then dry and frizzy-looking, screwed up into tight little curls, showing features that were all the plainer from her exceeding thinness and want of complexion".[3]

These two girls were destined to become Charlotte's greatest friends. It is from Charlotte's letters to Ellen Nussey that biographers have drawn most of their material, and for both of them Charlotte was to experience an affection which verged upon the sexual.

Ellen Nussey, the youngest of twelve, was the daughter of a cloth manufacturer's widow. She was a year younger than Charlotte and was considered to be pretty, though the sketch of her attributed to Charlotte shows a conventional chocolate-box beauty easy to forget. It is evident, however, that Ellen had character. Those who accuse her of the lack of it fail to consider that she had the intelligence to perceive the high qualities beneath the unprepossessing exterior of the little girl from the Parsonage.

Ellen began by comforting Charlotte during her bout of home-sickness, but their positions were soon reversed. It was Charlotte who guided, advised and protected the younger girl. Ellen occasionally patronized Charlotte, for she considered herself to be a cut above her friend in the social strata, but she openly acknowledged Charlotte's intellectual superiority.

Charlotte began to write to Ellen during the school vacation. Their early correspondence was conducted in schoolgirl French, but the laboured foreign notes soon became long, intimate revealing letters. Ellen must have valued them, because she kept them all.

In the early stage of their correspondence, the tone of Charlotte's letters was fervent, loving, verging upon the passionate. There can be no doubt that Charlotte had a 'crush' upon her friend.

She appears to have experienced a similar passion for Mary Taylor. Mary was also a member of a large and prosperous family, but was in character different to Ellen. Described by Miss Wooler as "too pretty to live", she was outspoken, intelligent and independent. She once described the Brontës as "like potatoes growing in a cellar", to which Charlotte answered meekly: "Yes, I know."

At school, Charlotte came into contact, for the first time, with girls who had been in different environments to her own. They also, to her chagrin, were more knowledgeable and thought her very ignorant and gauche. Yet they liked her. Charlotte was good-humoured and gentle, submitting upon one occasion to a game of ball, until her playmates realized that she could not see well enough to play. They liked her too because of her gift for telling stories.

The headmistress at first placed Charlotte in a lower class than her age warranted, but the new pupil felt the disgrace so bitterly that she was moved into a higher class and filled in the gaps in her knowledge with private study.

Charlotte even confided to her friends that she and her brother and sisters acted out plays and wrote stories, even promising to show them some. Later, reminded of that promise, she retracted it, saying she had been wrong to speak of it. Obviously, Charlotte was ready to admit her friends into the "infernal world", but to Branwell, Emily and Anne, who had not met them, the girls were strangers.

Even at Roe Head, Charlotte did not forget her dead sisters. She talked of them constantly, and told Mary of a dream she had had, in which Maria and Elizabeth, fashionably dressed, had come into the room and criticized the furniture. Later, in *Jane Eyre*, she was to describe another dream, in which she walked down a lonely road, hushing a dying child to sleep beneath her cloak. The old nightmare would always be there at the back of her mind, but the eighteen months she spent at Roe Head were happy ones.

If her eighteen months at Roe Head had been important, the next three years were equally so. During that period, all the

Brontës were at home together. Branwell was still under the tuition of his father, but Charlotte relieved her aunt of the burden of her sisters' education. She now passed on to Emily and Anne what she herself had learned. Charlotte, with her strong sense of duty, certainly intended to teach them, but if one is to judge from a diary paper of Emily's, neither of the girls assimilated very much grammar.

Written in appalling handwriting on a crumpled, blotted piece of paper, Emily's private note has puzzled biographers:

I fed Rainbow, Diamond Snowflake Jasper phaesant (alias) this morning Branwell went down to Mr Drivers and brought news that Sir Robert Peel was going to be invited to stand for Leeds Anne and I have been peeling apples for Charlotte to make an apple pudding and for aunts nuts and apples Charlotte said she made puddings perfectly and she was of a quick but limited intellect Taby said just now Come Anne pilloputate (i.e. pill a potato) Aunt has come into the kitchen just now and said where are your feet Anne Anne answered On the floor Aunt Papa opened the parlour door and gave Branwell a letter saying here Branwell read this and show it to your Aunt and Charlotte—The Gondals are discovering the interior of Gaaldine Sally Mosely is washing in the back-kitchen It is past twelve oclock Anne and I have not tidied ourselves, done our bed work or done our lessons and we want to go out to play we are going to have for Dinner Boiled Beef Turnips, potatoes and apple-pudding The kitchen is in a very untidy state Anne and I have not done our music exercise which consists of b major Taby said on my putting a pen in her face Ya pitter pottering there instead of pilling a potato I answered O dear O dear O dear I will directly with that I got up, take a knife and begin pilling (finished pilling the potatoes) papa going to walk Mr Sunderland expected.

Anne and I say I wonder what we shall be like if all goes well in the year 1874—in which year I shall be in my 57th year Anne will be going in her 55th year Branwell will be going in his 58th year and Charlotte in her 59th year hoping we shall all be well at that time we close our paper

Emily and Anne

November the 24th 1834.

Even if we make allowances for the fact that Emily wrote cramped up at the end of the kitchen table, the various members of the household interrupting her, the diary paper is still unbelievably childish for a girl of over sixteen years of age to have written. It does, however, give us an intimate picture of the Parsonage.

In 1833 Ellen Nussey visited the Parsonage for the first time. She evidently created a favourable impression, being the lady-like, tactful, gentle creature admired as an ideal by Mr Brontë and Aunt Branwell.[4] She was strongly attracted towards both Emily and Anne, leaving descriptions of them corroborated by the sketches drawn by Branwell about this time.

The holiday was apparently a great success. Aunt Branwell was in excellent spirits, taking snuff with an air of great daring and drawing upon her reminiscences of Cornwall for the amuse-ment of her youthful guest.

The girls spent most of their time out on the moors, taking Ellen to one of their favourite spots which they had christened "The Meeting of the Waters". Ellen recalled that Emily had waded through the streams, placing stepping stones for the others to tread upon, and had lain down by the side of the brook and tickled the trout there, with the unselfconscious pleasure of a child.

Of Branwell, Ellen had very little to say beyond the fact that he studied often with his father and that a career in paint-ing was being considered for him.

Few sixteen-year-old boys seek the company of their sisters, and Branwell was going through a phase of adolescent con-tempt for his own relatives. He described them as

miserable silly creatures not worth talking about. Charlotte's eighteen years old, a broad dumpy thing, whose head does not come higher than my elbow. Emily's sixteen, lean and scant, with a face about the size of a penny, and Anne is nothing, absolutely nothing.[5]

In the famous portrait Branwell painted of his sisters about this time, the girls appear to be gazing beyond the real world to the place beneath. Originally there were four figures in the group, but one has been smudged out, and for many years was believed to be a pillar, until X-ray examination showed it to be the figure of a man, presumably Branwell, who appar-ently disliked his likeness.

Charlotte is divided from the others, just as in life her fate was to be divided from theirs. She is square-faced and dumpy, as Branwell wrote of her, with a resolute expression.

On the other side of the canvas, Emily and Anne lean together, both looking in the same direction. They wear matching dresses, and their hair is bunched into corkscrew curls Their expressions are abstracted, almost trance-like, and they possess the same full-lipped, sensual mouths, so at variance with their other features.*

It is probably from this time also that the famous profile portrait of Emily dates. This too was one of a group, but the canvas was later mutilated by Mr Nicholls, who declared the likeness of Charlotte and Anne to be poor. From this, we can infer that the likeness of Emily is good. She still gazes out into space, and although the pose is erect, one has the impression that she is leaning forward, so intense is her glance.*

During their three years together in Haworth, many such groups must have been painted. Probably Branwell persuaded his father, his aunt and Tabby to sit for him. All such paintings have vanished. When he was not painting, or studying, he was writing, and when he was not writing, he was earning himself a reputation as a local wit, the golden boy of the village, the darling of the family, destined to bring them fame and fortune.

Nobody appears to have considered the talents of the girls. Sooner or later, they must earn their livings as governesses or teachers, the only profession open to a respectable young lady; in the meanwhile, they were not even allowed pocket-money. When Charlotte asked her father for some, he laughed and enquired what on earth she would do with it.[6]

Charlotte could have told him, but apparently did not, that with a little money she could have bought some dresses, instead of having to wear Aunt Branwell's home-made efforts. She could have paid for the postage of her letters, instead of Ellen having to pay the postage at the other end.[7] She could have enjoyed the feeling of independence which a little money bestows, and her need for independence was growing stronger. So too was her need for affection, but her abnormal shyness

* See illustrations.

held her back. She had inherited her father's reserve and his passionate nature.

Writing to Ellen in one letter, Charlotte tried to explain her feelings:

> I am very slow to believe the protestations of another, I know my own sentiments, I can read my own mind, but the minds of the rest of man and womankind are to me sealed volumes, hieroglyphical scrolls, which I cannot either unseal or decipher.

NOTES TO CHAPTER FOUR

1. Reminiscence of Ellen Nussey.
2. Letter from Mary Taylor to Mrs Gaskell.
3. Letter from Ellen Nussey to Mrs Gaskell.
4. Letter from Charlotte Brontë to Ellen Nussey.
5. *Angria and My Angrians*, paragraph attributed to Branwell Brontë.
6. Letter from Charlotte Brontë to Ellen Nussey.
7. Letter from Charlotte Brontë to Ellen Nussey.

FIVE

To the Sea

In 1835, Charlotte wrote to Ellen:

> We are about to divide, break up, separate. Emily is going to
> school, Branwell is going to London, and I am going to be a
> governess. This last determination I formed myself knowing that I
> should have to take a step sometime, "and better sune than
> syne", to use a Scottish proverb, and knowing well enough that
> Papa would have enough to do with his limited income, should
> Branwell be placed at the Royal Academy, and Emily at Roe
> Head . . . Emily and I leave home on the 27th of this month,
> the idea of being together consoles us both somewhat, and, in
> truth, since I must enter a situation, "my lines have fallen in
> pleasant places". I both love and respect Miss Wooler.

In fact, Charlotte had been invited to take a teaching post at
Roe Head by her old friend and headmistress. It was a friendly
gesture, destined to help Charlotte take her first steps in the
world, and Charlotte was grateful. Although she disliked the
idea of leaving home, she would be returning to a familiar
place and she would have Emily with her for company. But
within three months, Emily had been driven back to Haworth
by home-sickness.[1] Anne took her place at Roe Head, but the
sisters derived little comfort from each other.[2] Anne was four
years younger than Charlotte, and she was a pupil, whereas
Charlotte was now a member of the staff. They had little contact outside lessons, for Anne was naturally expected to par-

ticipate in the activities of the other girls, and Charlotte's evenings were taken up with the preparation of lessons and the marking of exercise books.

Charlotte had never particularly liked children and now she began positively to dislike them. Despite herself, she was forced sometimes to seize a pen and pour out her feelings:

> I am just going to write because I cannot help it. A. Cook on one side of me, E. Lister on the other, and Miss Wooler in the background. Stupidity the atmosphere, school books the employment, asses the society, what in all this is there to remind me of the divine, silent, unseen land of thought, dim now and indefinite as the dream of a dream, the shadow of a shade? . . . All Verdopolis came crowding into my mind. If I had had time to indulge it I felt that the vague sensation of the moment would have settled down into some narrative better at least than anything I have ever produced before. But just then a dolt came up with a lesson. I thought I should have vomited.

To be aware of one's powers but to lack the time in which to develop them, to be continually at the beck and call of others —such was her position. Such was her nature that she sought to blame herself for her own frustration. The secret world became for her, not only secret, but shameful. Her conscience informed her that to write down, even to picture, her deepest desires was sinful. Strictly conventional, fervently pious, Charlotte was sure, that anybody who saw such things as she did, must be damned.

To Ellen, she wrote:

> Don't deceive yourself by imagining that I have a bit of real goodness about me. My darling, if I were like you I should have to face zionwards. If you knew my thoughts; the dreams that absorb me; and the fiery imagination that at times eats me up and makes me feel society, as it is, wretchedly insipid, you would pity me and I daresay despise me.

What Ellen made of the letters is not known. Even in her, Charlotte could not fully confide, for Ellen knew nothing of Angria. If she ever guessed that more than her home-sickness and disappointment tormented her friend, she can hardly have said so.

Charlotte tried to channel some of her frustration off into

admiration of Ellen's spiritual qualities, but the depth of her despair and the intensity of her shame revealed itself.

If I could always live with you . . . I might one day become better, far better, than my evil wandering thoughts, my corrupt heart, cold to the spirit and warm to the flesh, will now permit me to be.

Yet even Ellen's religion failed to soothe Charlotte's conscience, which with its impossible demands forced her to face the shattering thought that she might be one of the damned.

Charlotte, obviously on the verge of a nervous breakdown, had new troubles with which to contend. In 1836, Emily took a post as teacher in Halifax,[3] and Charlotte, well aware of what absence from home could do to her sister, worried constantly about her.

During the summer vacation, Miss Wooler had moved her school from Roe Head to Dewsbury Moor. The new school buildings were smaller and the garden lacked the amenities of the former establishment. Within Heald House as it was called, Charlotte had even less privacy than before. In the late autumn of that year, Mrs Franks, née Frith, died suddenly. She had been Anne's godmother, had entertained the Brontës at Thornton, and had contributed towards the cost of their education. With her, Charlotte had been at ease, and her occasional visits to Roe Head had brightened the grinding monotony.

It needed a shock to jolt her out of the black apathy into which she had fallen. The shock was administered, unwittingly, by Anne. Anne had already suffered one bout of illness at Roe Head. This second attack began apparently as "a low fever", a convenient term which might refer to anything from gastritis to typhoid.

Charlotte was startled out of her own misery when she became aware of her sister's condition. Anne had a cough, a pain in her side, and experienced difficulty in breathing. All these were early symptoms of consumption, the disease dreaded by the Brontës, but Miss Wooler, when appealed to, declared frankly that Charlotte was making a fuss about nothing.

Charlotte immediately rounded upon the headmistress, and in her own words, "told her one or two plain truths, which set her a-crying, and the next day, unknown to me, she wrote to

Papa, telling him that I had reproached her bitterly . . . taken her severely to task, etc. etc. Papa sent for us the day after he had received the letter".[4]

Charlotte's quarrel with Miss Wooler was resolved before she went home. During their last interview, Miss Wooler seems to have apologized for her conduct and to have asked Charlotte to return as a governess. Charlotte agreed reluctantly to retain her post, and returned alone to Dewsbury in the New Year of 1838.

It was out of a sense of duty that she returned, and, relieved of her worst fears concerning Anne's health, trying to look upon the bright side in a poem written at that time.

> There's no use in weeping,
> Though we are condemned to part,
> There's such a thing as keeping
> A remembrance in one's heart.
> There's such a thing as dwelling
> On the thoughts ourselves have nursed,
> And with scorn and courage telling
> The world to do its worst.[5]

Despite these brave sentiments, Charlotte's state of mind worsened rapidly. Miss Wooler, wiser now than before, insisted that she consult a doctor, who advised her "as she valued her life to return home". At home again, Charlotte could return to the "infernal world", to steep herself in the romance and tragedy which brought such high delight. This is not to suggest that she spent an idle year. Indeed, there was rather more work than usual, for the family was temporarily without a servant. The previous Christmas, Tabitha had fallen and broken her leg. When Aunt Branwell decreed that she must be nursed in the village, her nieces resolved that as Tabby had cared for them in their youth, so they would care for her in old age. When argument failed, they went on hunger strike.[6] Emotional blackmail worked where reason did not and Tabby remained at the Parsonage.

When Charlotte came home finally from Dewsbury Moor, the Brontës were still without regular assistance, but shared the work cheerfully among themselves.

Mary Taylor and her younger sister, nineteen-year-old Martha, came to stay and their visit was a success. Mary was already a favoured friend, perhaps closer to Charlotte than Ellen, for although Ellen kept Charlotte's letters, Mary burnt the ones sent to her because she had no secure hiding place for such intimate documents.

Charlotte, climbing out of the black melancholia which had shattered her health, wrote:

They are making such a noise about me I cannot write any more. Mary is playing on the piano, Martha is chattering as fast as her little tongue can run, and Branwell is standing before her, laughing at her vivacity. A calm and even mind like yours cannot conceive the feelings of the shattered wretch who is now writing to you, when, after weeks of mental and bodily anguish not to be described, something like peace began to dawn again.[7]

The "shattered wretch" of twenty-two had long before accepted the unpalatable fact that she was plain, clumsy, and shy and therefore unlikely to marry. In her own small circle, however, her deficiencies were less noticeable. She had inherited her mother's fastidious neatness, possessed fine eyes, and, when she forgot her shyness, could talk fluently and vivaciously.

It was this vivacity, coupled with her intense femininity, that made her more attractive than she knew, and in the spring of 1839, Henry Nussey, Ellen's brother, proposed to Charlotte by letter.

Henry was a handsome, high-principled young man, who intended to become a missionary and had, unknown to Charlotte, drawn up a list of young ladies whom he deemed suitable[8] to be his wife. Having been refused by his first choice, he proceeded to the second. So far as Charlotte knew, it would be her only chance of matrimony, and the prospect was tempting. But even the thought of claiming Ellen as a sister-in-law could not overshadow the fact that no love existed between Henry Nussey and herself.

To Ellen, after refusing him, Charlotte wrote:

I could not sit all day long making a grave face before my husband. I would laugh and satirize, and say whatever came into my head first. And if he were a clever man, and loved me, the whole world weighed in the balance against his smallest wish should be as light as air. Could I, knowing my mind to be such as that, conscientiously take a grave, quiet young man such as Henry?

The Rev. Mr Nussey evidently received her refusal philosophically, noting in his diary: "Received an unfavourable reply from C.B. The Lord's will be done."

Charlotte's second proposal of marriage came from the Rev. Price, an Irish curate who visited the Parsonage and spent the evening chattering with her—they had just been introduced. A few days later, she received from him an offer of marriage.[9]

Obviously flattered, Charlotte treated the affair as a joke. Having turned away two prospective suitors, she could now say she was an old maid through choice rather than necessity.

In May 1839, Charlotte obtained a post with Mrs Sidgwick, of Stonegappe, near Skipton. To be a school teacher had been intolerable, but to be a private governess was infinitely worse.

The position of the governess in a Victorian family was a difficult one. She was not a servant, but was as poorly paid as one. She was usually far better educated than her employers, but was not a member of the family circle. Her entire day was at the beck and call of her charges, with her evenings usually spent in sewing, most employers expecting their governesses to help with the mending of lace and linen. If she was invited to eat with the family, etiquette decreed that she occupy the lowest place at table. When the family went driving, she took the least comfortable seat with its back to the horses, and nobody would have dreamed of helping her up to her place.

Charlotte, fully aware of her exceptional gifts, bitterly resented the patronage of people less intelligent than herself.

To Emily, she wrote:

The children are constantly with me. As for correcting them, I quickly found that was out of the question, they are to do as they like. . . . I said in my last letter that Mrs Sidgwick did not know me. I now begin to find that she does not intend to know me, that she cares nothing about me, except to contrive how the greatest possible quantity of labour may be squeezed out of me, and to that end she overwhelms me with oceans of needlework; yards of cambric to hem, muslin nightcaps to make, and, above all things, dolls to dress. I do not think she likes me at all, because I cannot help being shy in such an entirely novel scene, surrounded as I have hitherto been by strange and constantly changing faces. . . . I used to think I should like to be in the stir of grand folks' society; but I have had enough of it—it is dreary work to look on and listen. I see more clearly than I have ever done before, that a private governess has no existence, is not considered as a living, rational being, except as connected with the wearisome duties she has to fulfil.

Charlotte had this and more to bear, but she cannot have been an easy person to employ. The Sidgwicks declared that if they invited her to walk with them to church, she thought she was being treated like a slave. If they did not invite her, she considered herself slighted. She had no gift for imparting information and little patience with childish games. Above all, she possessed "no sense of gratitude".

That, in fact, was the crux of the matter. A governess was expected to be grateful to her employers for giving her a roof over her head, and Charlotte could not pretend to an emotion she did not feel. It is no surprise to hear that by the summer she had resigned her post with the thankful comment: "I was never so glad to get out of a place in my life."

Yet she knew, that if she were to maintain her independence, she must find another situation. There was absolutely no way in which she could expand her talents. Less than two years before she had sent some samples of her writing to Robert Southey, the Poet-Laureate; and to Wordsworth. Southey sent her "a cooling dose of admonition", and Wordsworth enquired sarcastically if she were "an attorney's clerk or a novel-reading dressmaker".[10]

Any hope she may have entertained of presenting her work to a wider public was crushed. The "cooling dose of admonition" did not, however, prevent her from continuing to write. Every spare moment was spent huddled over an exercise book, shaping anew the "infernal world". It was as potent as a drug, and as habit forming. To tear herself away must have required an incredible amount of will-power. Yet tear herself away Charlotte succeeded in doing. It is not known precisely when her *Farewell to Angria* was written, but it is believed to have been somewhere about this time.

It is also fairly certain that Charlotte did not break herself of the habit at once. It is difficult to suppress one's imagination, and she must have broken her resolve fairly often. But each excursion to the place beneath was followed by physical weariness and intense remorse.

It was perhaps during such a period that Ellen suggested they might go to the seaside together for a holiday. Charlotte welcomed the idea joyfully, for she had never seen the sea, and Ellen had friends near Bridlington with whom they could stay.

So deep is the gulf that separates Charlotte's world from our own that it is almost impossible to realize the daring of such a scheme. For two unmarried ladies, aged twenty-three and twenty-two respectively, to travel unchaperoned a distance of more than seventy miles, was almost unheard of.

Mr Brontë and Aunt Branwell were obviously shocked.

So many difficulties were put in the way, and so many objections voiced, that Charlotte lost hope.

The elders of the house have never cordially acquiesced in the measure, and now that impediments seem to start up at every step, opposition grows more open. Papa, indeed, would willingly indulge me, but this very kindness of his makes me doubt whether I ought to draw upon it; so, though I could battle out aunt's discontent, I yield to Papa's indulgence. He does not say so, but I know he would rather I stayed at home.

Ellen's reply to the foregoing measure was to borrow a friend's carriage and come to fetch Charlotte. The elders were so dumbfounded that she was permitted to leave at once and Branwell, delighting in his sister's rebellion, rushed about, making more noise than anybody as he shouted that "it was a brave defeat".

At Leeds, Charlotte entered a railway carriage for the first time in her life, and was in such a state of excitement, she was forced to remove her spectacles that she might not see the view too clearly.

They remained for a month with Ellen's friends, Mr and Mrs Hudson, and then went into lodgings in the town for a week until their money ran out.

Charlotte had always been fond of sketching and had even considered the possibility of selling some of her work. Unfortunately, the copying of one miniature took her six months, and brass rubbings from tombstones were not a popular form of interior decoration. Nevertheless, the occupation gave her great pleasure and while on holiday a large portion of her time was spent sketching.

Some of those sketches must surely have been of the sea. Her first reaction upon catching sight of it was to burst into tears. Ellen tactfully walked ahead, and within a few moments Charlotte caught up with her. Ellen recorded that she was still red-eyed and trembling, and for the remainder of the day scarcely spoke.

That first impression was never to leave her. All her life she was to be drawn to the sea in all its many moods, to describe it in her books, and to remember it with yearning.

NOTES TO CHAPTER FIVE

1. Mrs Gaskell, *Life of Charlotte Brontë*.
2. Derived from valid observations by Winifred Gerin in her biography, *Anne Brontë*.
3. Letter from Charlotte Brontë to Ellen Nussey.
4. Letter from Charlotte Brontë to Ellen Nussey.
5. Charlotte Brontë, 'Parting', written 29th January 1838.
6. Mrs Gaskell, *Life of Charlotte Brontë*.
7. Letter from Charlotte Brontë to Ellen Nussey.
8. Diary Papers of Henry Nussey.
9. Letter from Charlotte Brontë to Ellen Nussey.
10. Wordsworth's letter to Charlotte has not survived, but in her reply she quoted the words and apologized for having confused him.

SIX

Alias Northangerland

In 1835, Branwell had reached the age of eighteen years without ever having gone further from home than Leeds. All his life had been spent within the confines of Haworth, and his whole being yearned towards London. London was the Mecca of artists, writers, sculptors and politicians of every shade. Branwell bought a map of London, and pored over it for so long that, when a stranger mentioned a certain street, Branwell was able to inform him, without looking at the map, the most convenient way of getting there.[1]

This longing for London, did not mean that Branwell, at this stage, disliked his home. Not only did Mr Brontë keep his son away from school, but Branwell himself expressed no desire to go there. School was bound up with memories of his adored Maria, and no doubt Charlotte's own account of Cowan Bridge must have made him all the more thankful that he was to remain at home.

It is evident that he spent a great portion of his time with his father. He used the same phrases as Mr Brontë and had acquired the latter's habit of addressing even close friends as 'Sir'. How Branwell spent his time when his lessons were finished, was considered to be his own affair. Much of that free time was devoted, with Charlotte's collaboration, to the writing of the minute booklets, but his sister's company was not completely sufficient, and Branwell liked, quite naturally, to play with other boys, to chat with the villagers, and to pay a never-to-be forgotten visit to the Fair at Keighley.[2]

At eighteen, Branwell, small and be-spectacled, was possessed, according to everyone who ever met him, with inordinate charm. The well-known profile portrait medallion of him by J. B. Leyland hardly corresponds to contemporary ideas of masculine beauty, but Branwell was evidently one of those people who become more attractive when they are mobile. In repose, the beaked nose, receding chin and puckered eyebrows are unprepossessing, but those who knew Branwell spoke of his lively expression, graceful figure and beautiful speaking voice.[3]

Unlike his sisters, Branwell was high-spirited and gregarious, with a liking for practical jokes and a seemingly extrovert nature. His talents were spectacular. He played the organ with dash, and became so excited upon hearing music that he would beat time wildly on the furniture. His literary output was already tremendous and his paintings had impressed his art master, William Robinson, so much that the whole family expected Branwell to be a great artist.

There were other, almost eccentric gifts that earned him something of a local reputation. He wrote simultaneously with both hands, sometimes writing in Greek with the left hand, and in Latin with the right hand. He invented a language consisting of Cornish, Irish and Yorkshire dialect with Latin endings; the Brontës spoke this invented speech as fluently as English.

Branwell's own flow of conversation was so inexhaustible, that, if a stranger put up for the night at the 'Black Bull', the landlord would offer to run up to the Parsonage and fetch 'Patrick' to provide some entertainment.[4]

In the village, the parson's son was known as 'Patrick'; at home, he was referred to always as Branwell. To the girls he was 'Young Soult'. 'Patrick Benjamin Wiggins', 'Chief Genius Brannii'. 'The Earl of Northangerland, alias Rogue, alias Alexander Percy'.

The decision to send him to the Royal Academy in London was apparently unanimous. In London, Branwell would acquire the technical skill that he lacked, and would be in the midst of an artistic, cosmopolitan society. He might earn commissions while he studied, or a wealthy art collector might decide to become his patron.

Branwell left Haworth for London in the October of that year.[5] His fees were paid by Mr Brontë and by Aunt Branwell, who adored her nephew. What happened in London is not certain, but within a month Branwell was back in Haworth, without, apparently, having submitted his sketches or letters of introduction to the Academy.

The story current in Haworth at that time was that he had been waylaid by highwaymen and robbed. If it were true, the family kept remarkably silent about the affair. The subject was never mentioned again, and this reticence suggests that whatever befell Branwell in London was of a disreputable nature.

From henceforth, while identifying himself passionately with the amoral Northangerland, he wrote of his other self from a purely feminine viewpoint. As Harriet, he wrote:

> Oh, I led a life of sinning
> At her beck, whose soul was sin;
> Yet my spirit ceased repining
> If a look from him 'twould win'
> Bright that band with hellish glory
> Circling round Augusta's throne,
> Dark those hearts whose influence o'er me,
> Led me in and lured me on.[6]

It is dangerous to draw too close a line between the language of poetry and the language of experience, but in 'Harriet's' account, the young lady appears sadly confused as to the sex of her loved one!

During the whole of 1836, Branwell is believed to have remained in Haworth where most of his time was occupied in writing. Emily, released from Roe Head, had more of the disposal of her own time, and during this period brother and sister inevitably spent a great part of their leisure together.

Branwell, however, always needed a wider audience. His friends in the village provided one. A regular visitor at the 'Black Bull', he was also a member of the Temperance Society, thus his drinking probably stopped short at a glass of ale. Certainly, there was no gossip in the village concerning his habits, and his character was so highly regarded that he was initiated into the Masonic Society when still under the minimum age.

The Brontë Sisters, a painting by Branwell Brontë, *circa* 1835

Charlotte Brontë, by
George Richmond, 1851

Branwell Brontë, the
medallion by Joseph
Leyland

Branwell's sponsor was John Brown, the sexton, one of his closest friends and one often declared to be the cause of Branwell taking to drink. Brown could, admittedly, hold a vast quantity of liquor, and possessed a magnificently blasphemous vocabulary, but he could also swop Latin and Greek tags with Mr Brontë, was well liked at the Parsonage, and was happily married with six little girls. His portrait, painted by Branwell, is of a burly, full-faced man, with intelligence and sensuality mingled in his expression.[7]

Like Charlotte, Branwell was not content to write purely for his own pleasure, and to do him justice, was far less easily discouraged. Throughout that year he wrote constantly to editor after editor in the hope of interesting somebody in his work. His great ambition was to contribute to *Blackwood's Magazine*, and to this end he sent dozens of stories and poems, accompanied by long, boastful letters, whining letters, filed in the archives of the publishing house because they were "amusing".

Like his elder sister he sent a poem to Wordsworth, but the ageing poet ignored it, declaring the accompanying letter to be "disgusting".[8]

The letter was dated 19th January 1837, and concluded:

Do pardon me, sir, that I have ventured to come before one whose works I have most loved in our literature, and who most has been with me a divinity of the mind, laying before him one of my writings, and asking of him a judgement of its contents. . . . Now, to send you the whole of this would be a mock of your patience; what you see does not pretend to be more than the description of an imaginative child. But read it, sir, and as you would hold a light to one in utter darkness—as you value your own kindheartedness—*return me an answer* if but one word, telling me if I should write on or write no more.[9]

The one word was never written, but Branwell continued to submit his work though he was beginning to despair of ever making a name for himself.

Mr Brontë underlined in his copy of *Modern Domestic Medicine*, a remedy for intoxication: "12 drops of pure water of ammonia, taken in a wine glass of milk and water, repeated in ten minutes and again in half-an-hour."[10] In the margin by the date 1837, he had written: "Cold water may answer best B."

D

Branwell, increasingly frustrated, must have been spending more time than usual at the 'Black Bull'. If he did return home slightly the worse for wear sometimes, no outsiders seemed to notice anything.

Branwell, himself, certainly did not consider drink to be a problem. A few glasses of ale or gin would restore him to his usual high spirits, lift the constant, humiliating shadow of failure. Coupled with this was his overwhelming sense of sin.

Other people might see him as "t'parson's Patrick", but he saw himself as Northangerland, incarnation of evil. For such a character, there could be no redemption. Branwell would never rejoin Maria who was in Heaven, and rather than face that possibility, he preferred to deny the existence of Heaven.

> We say this world was made for One
> Who's seen or heard by none.
> We say that He, the Almighty God
> That framed Creation with a nod.
> His wondrous work so well fulfilled
> That—in an hour—it All rebelled.
> That though He loves our race so well
> He hurls our spirits into Hell—
> That though He bids us turn from sin
> He hedges us with tempters in—
> That though He says the world shall stand
> Eternal—perfect—from His hand,
> He's just about to whelm it o'er
> With utter ruin—evermore!
> And all for deeds that we have done
> Though He has made us every one!
> Yes, WE—the image of His form!
> We! The dust to feed the worm![11]

Early in 1838 Branwell left Haworth again and went to Bradford, with the intention of earning his living as a freelance painter.

Bradford, thriving cloth centre, was also the pivot of a vivid artistic circle, inhabited by several writers, among them William Dearden, "the bard of Caldene", who later thought so highly of Branwell's powers that he believed him capable of writing *Wuthering Heights*. In Bradford, also, were the Leyland brothers. Joseph, the elder, was, at twenty-six years of age, an already famous sculptor, who had exhibited in Manchester and Leeds. He took the boy from Haworth under his wing, but as Leyland himself was an alcoholic, this may not have been such an advantage.

Branwell lodged with Mr and Mrs Kirby, in Rainbow Street, renting a sudio there, and walking home across the moors at weekends. Margaret Hartley, the Kirby's niece, declared that the parson's son was a sober, well-conducted young gentleman and remembered how Branwell had taken a fancy to one of the Kirby children, insisting that the child and himself should take their meals together.

Branwell may have given Miss Hartley a favourable impression, but nobody else was sufficiently attracted by the newcomer to commission him to paint their portraits. His pictures of Mr and Mrs Kirby were probably executed in lieu of rent.[12] Notoriously generous, Branwell was going through a phase of sartorial perfection, with top hat at a jaunty angle, pale grey trousers, and smart cane.[13] Aunt Branwell was financing him but was in no danger of being repaid for her kindness. Branwell must have felt qualms of conscience, but it was easier to drown conscience in a glass of gin than to go touting for custom.

Branwell had been scarcely a year in Bradford, when Mr Brontë called him home. Whether his father had heard disturbing reports of his conduct is not known. There is a possibility, however, that Branwell's health was again causing concern. Mr Brontë had pencilled in the letter B, and the date 1838, beside the paragraph headed "Nightmare", in his copy of Modern Domestic Medicine. A little further on in the book is another marginal comment. By the side of the words "tic doloroux", Mr Brontë noted that the words signified "a painful convulsive fit".

Francis Leyland wrote later that during a trip to Liverpool undertaken early in 1839, Branwell had "an attack of tic, which compelled him to resort to opium".

Leyland was not among the party who visited Liverpool and his story has been doubted by biographers, but then he had not seen Mr Brontë's copy of Modern Domestic Medicine either, and it seems very likely that Branwell had begun to suffer again from epilepsy.

Opium, in the form of laudanum, was then easily obtainable. It was used as a general sedative by everybody, was even recommended for fretful babies, and was said to be a preventive against consumption. It could be bought in any pharmacy for a few pence, and it left no tell-tale odour on the breath. Moreover, poets like Coleridge used it experimentally, seeking to sharpen their perceptions that they might attain to a higher plane of aesthetic consciousness.

For Branwell it represented escape from the constant rejections of his manuscripts, the lack of commissions for his portraits, the shortage of money, and the crushing sense of sin as he moved further away from the ideals of his childhood.

By 1839, Branwell was at home again and, according to Charlotte, in high good humour. He enjoyed the company of the Taylor girls, and, according to popular tradition, Mary Taylor fell in love with him. The match would have been an excellent one, for the strong-minded, beautiful girl might have proved exactly the kind of wife he needed.

Northangerland would have seduced Mary without a second's hesitation and Branwell fancied himself in the role of seducer. He probably paid her marked attentions, but when Mary took them seriously, Branwell panicked. Northangerland vanished, and an extremely uneasy young man treated her with marked coldness.

Charlotte, in a letter to Ellen Nussey, some months later, mentioned the affair.

Did I not once tell you of an instance of a relative of mine who cared for a young lady until he began to suspect that she cared more for him and then instantly conceived a sort of contempt for her? You know to what I allude. Never as you value your life mention the circumstances—Mary is my study—for the contempt, the remorse, the misconstruction which follow the development of feelings in themselves noble, warm, generous, devoted and profound, but which, being too freely revealed, too frankly bestowed, are not estimated at their real value.[14]

How deep Mary's affections ran cannot, of course, be judged. Charlotte may have read more into the glances of her friend than ever existed, but it is significant that Mary and Martha seldom visited the Parsonage after that summer. She was, indeed, destined to remain a spinster, whether from lack of offers or from choice is not known.

Branwell's conduct in the affair, however, was typical. So long as his lady-love assumed no tangible form he was perfectly content. In the "infernal world" he kept dozens of mistresses, sharing among them his superhuman virility. In the Parsonage, he took one look at a flesh-and-blood woman, and fled.

It was becoming increasingly evident to Branwell that the real world held too many terrors. He could not face it without the artificial reliefs of drink and opium, and this fact was one that he must not admit, least of all to himself.

NOTES TO CHAPTER SIX

1. Haworth local tradition.
2. Haworth local tradition.
3. Description by Francis Leyland.
4. Haworth local tradition.
5. Letter from Charlotte Brontë to Ellen Nussey.
6. Branwell Brontë, *Angrian Saga*.
7. *John Brown*, portrait by Branwell Brontë.
8. Reported remark by Wordsworth to Southey.
9. Letter from Branwell Brontë to Wordsworth.
10. *Modern Domestic Medicine*—annotated copy now at Haworth Parsonage Museum.
11. Branwell Brontë, 'Azreal'.
12. Portraits of Mr and Mrs Kirby, now at Haworth Parsonage Museum.
13. Charlotte Brontë, *Angria and My Angrians*—description of Patrick Benjamin Wiggins.
14. Letter from Charlotte Brontë to Ellen Nussey.

SEVEN

Emily Alone

In 1835, Emily Brontë was seventeen years old, an age praised in song and proverb as one of the most pleasant periods of one's life. At seventeen years of age, most girls have overcome the problems of adolescence, but are not yet burdened with the responsibilities of maturity.

It was at this age that Emily left home to become a pupil at Roe Head. Within three months she had returned to Haworth. Charlotte wrote:

> The change from her own home to a school, and from her own very noiseless, very secluded, but unrestricted and unartificial mode of life, to one of disciplined routine (though under the kindest auspices) was what she failed in enduring. Her nature proved too strong for her fortitude. Every morning, when she woke, the vision of home and the moors rushed on her, and darkened and saddened the day before her. Nobody knew what ailed her but I knew only too well. In this struggle her health was quickly broken, her white face, attenuated form, and failing strength threatened rapid decline. I felt in my heart she would die, if she did not go home, and with this conviction obtained her recall.[1]

Certainly, Emily was deeply attached to her home and to the surrounding moors, where she spent so much of her leisure time. Away from the heath with which she identified herself so closely, her feelings were akin to those of a prisoner.

What language can utter the feeling
That rose, when in exile afar,
On the brow of a lonely hill kneeling
I saw the brown heath growing there.
It was scattered and stunted, and told me
That soon even that would be gone;
It whispered "The grim walls enfold me",
I have bloomed in my last summer's sun.[2]

Yet other girls have suffered from home-sickness without reaching a point where their relatives consider them to be in danger of death. Undoubtedly, the loss of Maria must have been a profound emotional shock to the six-year-old Emily, but the shock remained unexpressed. Charlotte and Branwell, particularly Branwell, returned again and again to the theme of the death of a young girl. Emily does not appear to have displayed her grief in this obvious fashion. None of her childish writings have survived, but her later poems equate death with a separation from one's natural environment.

Even this cannot fully explain her abnormal clinging to familiar surroundings. Outwardly, Emily was supremely normal. She was described as "the pet nursling" of Cowan Bridge, and by Tabby as "the tallest and the prettiest. A darling of a child."

Mr Brontë related that Emily quarrelled violently with Branwell when Branwell teased Anne, and that Emily was punished on one occasion for climbing out of the study window and snapping a branch off a tree outside.

Emily was, to all intents and purposes, then, a lively, affectionate girl who fought with her brother and got up to mischief when her father's back was turned. She was easily the most gifted of the family. Her sketches of her pets leap out of their frames, so vibrant are they.[3] She was reported by Ellen Nussey to have reached a professional standard of excellence in the art of playing the piano. Nor were domestic tasks neglected. Emily not only took an active part in the housework, but enjoyed cooking and scrubbing, while the needlework she executed was of incredible delicacy. Her nature was, according to Charlotte, practical. Later on, it was Emily who managed the household accounts and invested the family savings in railway shares. It was Emily whom Aunt Branwell scolded for her unladylike habits of whistling and using slang expressions.[4]

In her own environment of Haworth, Emily was completely normal to outward appearance. Yet her poems, written in secret and shown only to Anne, reveal a side of her personality greatly at variance with the self she presented to the world. They describe, or attempt to describe, a profound emotional experience which can never be forgotten but returns even in sleep.

> O God of Heaven! The dream of horror,
> The frightful dream is over now;
> The sickening heart, the blasting sorrow,
> The ghastly night, the ghastlier sorrow,
> The aching sense of utter woe.[5]

All of Emily's surviving poems can be fitted into her Gondal saga. This has led many critics and biographers to the conclusion that the poems do not arise from personal experience at all. This is surely as great a misconception as to declare all her work to be a literal account of actual events.

As is obvious from Emily's first diary paper, between Gondal and herself was no sharp division. Charlotte and Branwell escaped to the place beneath as a refuge from reality. Emily carried Gondal about within herself and the course of events there must have been influenced to a certain extent by events and changes in the real world.

Either Emily described imaginary situations so brilliantly that they were believed to be actual experiences, or she wrote of real experiences in terms of Gondal. Her extreme reserve could thus control her longing to find relief in the writing out of her feelings.

There are two themes implicit in Emily's work. The first is an emotional horror, as if she suffered some devastating experience quite early in life that haunted her throughout her days. It has been suggested that she saw her 'animus', or second self.[6] This experience is sometimes held to be symptomatic of a disturbed mind, but this does not explain why there are recorded instances of the second self being seen by impartial observers.

If Emily's conscious and unconscious selves pulled so far in different directions that they assumed separate physical entities, one can understand why she would seek to remain in a familiar place, and why the dread of discovery would effectually curtail her attempts to live in the outside world.

Later, her poems suggest that she was able to harness this elemental power in order to bring her soul closer to the Infinite. It is generally agreed that she practised mysticism and achieved union with the Absolute—chief aim of mystic experiment—to a very high degree.

> Listen! tis just the hour,
> The awful time for thee.
> Dost thou not feel upon thy soul
> A flood of strange sensations roll,
> Forerunners of a sterner power,
> Heralds of me?[7]

Conventionally reared, Emily evolved for herself a philosophy in which the bigotry of Charlotte and the hopelessness of Anne had no part. It was a creed which denied creed, a pantheistic view of eternal life, which must, inevitably, have taken great energy and determination to formulate. It was a creed which had to be worked out in silence and solitude. Only at Haworth could she achieve this necessary detachment from the external world, while continuing to fulfil her earthly obligations.

These two sides of Emily's nature—the contemplative and the practical—do not indicate any degree of schizophrenia.

One of the greatest mystics of all time, St Teresa of Avila, ran her convents with extreme efficiency, enjoyed hard manual work, and told a group of dreamy-faced novices: "We don't want any more saints here. We want some good scrubbers."[8]

It was a sentiment with which Emily would have heartily concurred. Nobody was ever able to accuse her of neglecting her duties or of day-dreaming. She deliberately disciplined herself to obey the small rules of household management, in much the same way as a nun must practise complete obedience to the external rules of her Order before she can hope to achieve a complete submerging of her will with the Will of God.

This complete abandonment of one's personality until it is absorbed into the Divine is considered to be mystical experience. The ecstasy of such union is usually expressed in terms of sexual satisfaction, because mystics have no expressions to exactly denote their experiences. It is an experience in which the soul leaves the body, and it has definite physical aspects. The person undergoing the ecstasy falls into an apparent trance during which their body becomes rigid, their eyes glazed, their heartbeats slower. In this state, induced with great difficulty, they neither see nor hear. A physician, called to examine St Bernadette of Lourdes, burned her fingers with a candle and declared that not only was there no nervous reaction to the pain, but that the skin remained unscorched.[9]

When the experience ends, the soul returns, as it were, to the body with immense reluctance. As a mystic becomes aware of his return to the external world, he experiences a sense of loss so agonizing that it becomes a physical pain.

> Oh, dreadful is the check, intense the agony
> When the ear begins to hear and the eye begins to see;
> When the pulse begins to throb, the brain to think again,
> The soul to feel the flesh and the flesh to feel the chain![10]

This is not to suggest that Emily Brontë was a saint. No saint would take pleasure in leading her timid sister close to strange animals and then mocking her fears, as Emily did to Charlotte. No saint would be so obstinate that if her family wished her to do something, they could achieve their aims only by begging her to do the opposite.[11]

Emily's intensely private experiences were not due to a nature of holiness. Neither did she achieve her state of rapture at once. She was to undergo another emotional experience which has not yet been explained.

In 1836 Emily left Haworth for the second time. She became a school mistress in Miss Patchett's Academy at Law Hill, Halifax. Whether Emily herself decided to conquer her homesickness, or whether the family urged her, is not known.[12] Neither is it known exactly how long she stayed there.

Charlotte wrote to Ellen:

> My sister Emily is gone into a situation as a teacher in a large school of near forty pupils, near Halifax. I have had one letter since her departure; it gives an appalling account of her duties. Hard labour from six in the morning until near eleven at night, with only one half-hour of exercise between. This is slavery. I fear she will never stand it.[13]

The account is so incredible that one is inclined to believe that Emily, whether leaving home of her own accord or not, was already preparing the grounds for her return. Some of her finest poetry was written between November 1837, and May 1840. Embedded in the 'Gondal Saga', it has also been held to be a poetical record of Emily's own experiences.

> The night is darkening round me,
> The wild winds coldly blow;
> But a tyrant spell has bound me
> And I cannot, cannot go.[14]

The spell binding Emily to Law Hill is believed to have been that of love. To say this is in no way to depreciate her genius. Nobody thinks any the worse of Charlotte because her unsatisfied sexual yearnings found expression in Angria; but of late, a howl of protest is heard when it is suggested that Emily's Gondal poems arise from her personal feelings.

The theme of Emily's poems written during, and for some time after, her sojourn at Law Hill is that of rejection. The poet, under a variety of Gondal pseudonyms, falls passionately in love but is severed from the object of her affections, and mourns so intensely that the separation becomes a kind of death.

> I'll not weep that thou art going to leave me,
> There's nothing lovely here;
> And doubly will the dark world grieve me
> While thy heart suffers there.

A fortnight later, Emily was writing :

> If grief for grief can touch thee,
> If answering woe for woe,
> If any truth can melt thee,
> Come to me now.
> Yes, by the tears I've poured thee,
> By all my hours of pain,
> O, I shall surely win thee,
> Beloved, again.[15]

The object of Emily's affection has never been discovered. Neither is it known to what extent the affair reached actuality.

A powerful and sensitive imagination may build a whole world on a casual glance or a carelessly chosen phrase.

It has been suggested that Emily fell in love with a member of her own sex.[16] Certainly she was not a 'feminine' woman, for according to the villagers of Haworth, she "walked like a man and had a deep, husky voice".

She was personally untidy, unlike her sisters who were almost dainty, and she wandered about in long, lank skirts, which she never bothered to lift when crossing a brook. It was Emily, not Branwell, who held shooting competitions with Mr Brontë against the church wall,[17] and Charlotte remembered, innocently, that her sister habitually referred to herself as "a gay, young fellow".

Yet a girl may do all these things and still be free of the taint of Lesbianism. Moreover, there is during adolescence a perfectly natural tendency for a girl to be attracted towards a member of her own sex. It is a normal phase of emotional growth which fades away to be replaced by heterosexual passions.[18]

If a supernatural shock in childhood had led to an early flowering of her intellectual and spiritual qualities, it could have just as easily retarded her social and sexual development. Emily might, therefore, have reached the homosexual phase far later than most, and, being profoundly religious, have suffered tremendous psychological disturbance.

In those pre-Freudian days, she would have interpreted her own feelings as sinful. Nothing else can explain her determined isolation from the world, her refusal even to talk to outsiders. If she had, in addition, been actually rejected by a member of her own sex, she might deliberately repress her unnatural urges, believing them to be permanent, and sublimate her instincts in mystical union.

At some point during her stay at Law Hill, she screamed at her class that she thought more of the yard-dog than of them. This attitude was to become even stronger as the years went by. In her poems, emotion is poured out upon the beauties of Nature and upon certain mystical experiences, but Emily resolutely held aloof from her own kind.

Of Emily, Charlotte was to write:

"Stronger than a man and simpler than a child, her nature stood alone."[19]

In those words, Charlotte came closer than any other biographer in summing up the essential quality of her sister's strange, solitary genius.

NOTES TO CHAPTER SEVEN

1. Charlotte Brontë, Biographical Notice on Emily Brontë.
2. Emily Brontë, 'Loud without the wind was roaring', 11th November 1838.
3. See sketch of Keeper in Haworth Parsonage Museum.
4. Charlotte used these habits of Emily to create the personality of her heroine in Shirley.
5. Poem by Emily Brontë, August 1837.
6. Philip Henderson, Introduction to the Poems of Emily Brontë (the Folio Society).
7. Emily Brontë, 'I'll come when thou art saddest', circa 1837.
8. Frances Parkinson Keyes, 'Life of St Teresa of Avila', from Land of Stones and Saints.
9. Herbert Thurston, SJ, The Physical Phenomena of Mysticism (Burns and Oates, 1958).
10. Emily Brontë, 'Julian M. and G. Rochelle', October 1845.
11. Mrs Gaskell, Life of Charlotte Brontë.
12. In her Biographical Notice, Charlotte wrote: "It was some time before the experiment of sending her from home was again ventured upon."
13. Letter from Charlotte Brontë to Ellen Nussey, October 1836.
14. Emily Brontë, poem, November 1837.
15. Emily Brontë, poem, May 1840.
16. Somerset Maugham in his Ten Greatest Novels.
17. The bullet holes are still pointed out to visitors.
18. Sigmund Freud, Psychogenesis of a case of Homosexuality in a Woman; Certain Neurotic Mechanisms in Jealousy, Paranoia and Homosexuality.
19. Charlotte Brontë, Biographical Notice.

EIGHT

Anne

In 1835, Anne Brontë replaced Emily at Roe Head school, when home-sickness forced the latter to return to Haworth.

The tradition has arisen that Anne, too, suffered intensely during her period of schooling. Certainly she missed her home, and missed, even more, the companionship of her sister Emily. Ellen Nussey said they were "like twins". However, the picture of Anne as a gentle, timid shrinking female has been over-drawn. For this, Charlotte must in part be blamed. Anne, to her sister, was the baby of the family, to be protected against the world. Unconsciously, Charlotte consistently underestimated her strength of character and presented to the world a sweet, shadowy, insipid young girl who flits through the Brontë story like a wraith.[1]

Anne was undoubtedly delicate. Her nickname in the family was 'Old Asthma', so it is evident that she suffered from that distressing complaint so often associated with nervous trouble. There is also ample evidence that the Methodism of her aunt exercised great influence over her mind. All through her life, her natural gaiety was to be overshadowed by the dread of damnation!

It has become the fashion to interpret Anne's poems as purely autobiographical, but to take each sentiment expressed as a literal one is to underestimate the power of Gondal. Both Emily and Anne played constantly at Gondal, and although it never

became for the younger girl what it was to become for her
sister, many of Anne's poems fit very comfortably into the
'Gondal Saga'. Her earliest poem to be preserved, dated 1836,
is usually taken to be autobiographical. In that year Anne became a pupil at Roe Head school. The lines

> I will leave thee then my childhood's home,
> For all the joys are gone,
> I leave thee through the world to roam
> In search of fair renown.
> From such a hopeless home to part
> Is happiness to me,
> For nought can charm my weary heart
> Except activity.[2]

are usually thought to express Anne's own feelings upon going
to school.

Quite apart from the fact that the poem is called 'Verses by
Lady Geralda', common sense alone would inform us that while
the poet, like Anne, is leaving home, any further resemblance
between reality and fiction must exist only in the wishful
thinking of the biographer.

Anne's childhood home was certainly not a joyless place.
Those who quote the verses as evidence of Anne's striving to
leave her environment, overlook the fact that the verses themselves betray extreme dissatisfaction with home life. In 1835,
Branwell was on the verge of what his family fondly believed
would be a distinguished artistic career. There was, as yet, no
shadow of unhappiness over the Parsonage.

Greatly as she disliked leaving Emily, Anne must have been
fully aware of the advantages that further education would
bring. At Roe Head she would be able to advance her knowledge and polish her accomplishments. Later, she was fully
qualified to teach French, German and Latin, in addition to the
music and sketching in which she took such reputed pleasure.

Unfortunately, Anne's period at school corresponded with
Charlotte's long attack of neurasthenia. Charlotte trapped in her
own religious difficulties, tormented by the gnawing conscience
which made every pleasure of the infernal world a heinous
sin, apparently wasted no time in helping Anne to settle down.
The girl, who had never been away from home in her life,

had to adapt herself speedily to the school routine. She succeeded in doing so to such an extent that she won a prize for
good conduct at the end of her first year.* But her struggles
were silent and lonely, for there is every reason to suppose that
Charlotte and Anne had little contact outside normal lesson
hours.

Inevitably, her physical condition deteriorated, and she became seriously ill with gastro-enteritis.† In her weakened condition she believed herself to be dying and asked that a minister
should be brought. To this minister she confided her dread of
damnation, and her fear that she would never attain that perfection, without which, salvation is impossible. The Rev. James
La Trobe was exactly the right type of person to help Anne.
By nature practical and cheerful, he was able to convince her
of the truth of Divine Mercy.[3] The meeting made a deep impression upon her. Although religious melancholy was to attack
her time and time again, she never lost sight of her conviction
that Salvation is possible for all.

> With this polluted heart
> I dare to come to Thee,
> Holy and mighty as Thou art,
> For Thou will pardon me.

During the summer holidays, Emily and Anne wrote out together a diary paper.

Monday evening, 26th June 1837

A bit past 4-o-clock Charlotte working in Aunt's room, Branwell reading Eugene Aram to her—Anne and I writing in the
drawing room—Anne a poem beginning "Fair was the evening
and brightly the sun"—I Augustus—Almeda's Life 1st v. 1–4th
page from the last. Fine rather coolish then grey cloudy but
sunny day. Aunt working in the little room Papa gone out Tabby
in the kitchen The Emperors and Empresses of Gondal and Gaaldine preparing to depart from Gaaldine to Gondal to prepare for
the coronation which will be on the 12th of July Queen Vittoria
ascended the throne this month. Northangerland in Monkey's
Isle—Zamorna at Evesham. All tight and right in which condition it is to be hoped we shall all be this day 4 years at which
time Charlotte will be 25 and 2 months Branwell just 24 it being

---

* The prize was *On the Improvement of the Mind*.
† It was actually termed a "low fever" or "gastric trouble".

Anne Brontë, painted by
Charlotte Brontë, *circa*
1834

Emily Brontë, painted by
Branwell Brontë, *circa*
1835

(*left*) Mr Brontë, aged
fifty-six. (*below*) Haworth
Parsonage in 1853. The
figure in the background
is believed to be
Charlotte Brontë

his birthday—myself 22 and 10 months and a piece Anne 21 and nearly a half I wonder where we shall be and how we shall be and what kind of day it will be then let us hope for the best.

Emily Jane Brontë—Anne Brontë.

I guess that this day 4 years we shall all be in this drawing-room comfortable I hope it may be so. Anne guessed we shall all be gone somewhere together comfortable. We hope it may be so indeed.

The diary paper, illustrated by a sketch of Emily and Anne writing, gives more than a hint of insecurity. As a frightened child in a darkened room will enumerate the various items of furniture, so Emily and Anne carefully record everyone's whereabouts and end on a note of optimism, as if it were a talisman against ill-fortune.

A few weeks later, Anne was back at school, deprived of Emily's company and set down in Heald House at Dewsbury Moor. Charlotte, possibly temporarily revived at home, sank back into her black apathy. Anne was forced to make new adjustments, again without help or encouragement, but this second adaptation proved too much for her health. She caught a severe cold which rapidly became worse and jolted Charlotte out of her uninterested attitude.

Anne was rushed back to Haworth by her panic-stricken sister, who, having blamed Miss Wooler for her "indifference", imagined that the symptoms of tuberculosis were already apparent. She may have been more correct than she knew. Anne's frame always delicate, was probably already the harbourer of tubercular germs.

The family were evidently content for this youngest girl to remain quietly at home, but Anne wished to earn her own living. Unlike Charlotte and Emily, she was fond of children, and thought she would enjoy teaching them.[4]

She obtained a post, probably through Miss Wooler's recommendation, with the Ingham family of Blake Hall, near Mirfield. The Brontës evidently protested, but Anne was determined to stand on her own feet and won a grudging consent from her father to leave home.

Mirfield was the neighbourhood in which Roe Head school had been situated, so the district was already familiar. The Inghams were wealthy and respectable, with strong Methodist

E

connections, and Mr Brontë was assured by Miss Wooler that Mrs Ingham was "a very nice woman".

Anne left home on 8th April 1839, and a week later Charlotte wrote to Ellen:

> Poor child, she left us last Monday, no one went with her, it was her own wish that she might be allowed to go alone, as she thought she could manage better and summon more courage if thrown entirely upon her own resources. We have had one letter from her since she went.

The letter continues, patronizingly:

> You would be astonished what a sensible, clever letter she writes, it is only the talking part I fear. But I do seriously apprehend that Mrs Ingham will sometimes conclude that she has a natural impediment in her speech.[5]

For Charlotte, the nineteen-year-old girl was still a baby sister to be protected, cherished and underestimated. Charlotte was even surprised that Anne could compose a coherent letter.

Blake Hall was a large house, standing in its own extensive grounds. There were five children, three of whom were in Anne's charge—a boy of six, and two girls aged five years and three years.

Anne described her pupils as "desperate little dunces", unable to recount the alphabet. They were also excessively spoilt, for Mr and Mrs Ingham believed in free expression, and their precious darlings were allowed to do exactly as they pleased. According to Anne's own account, it pleased them to spit in her handbag and fling its contents out of the window, to throw food at one another during mealtimes and to drop like stones to the ground when their governess called them to lessons.

On one occasion, they ran out of the schoolroom and rode away on their ponies, leaving Anne weeping in the courtyard. Another time the children discovered a nest of fledglings and proceeded to tell Anne how they intended to torture them to death. Knowing that a struggle would wreak more harm than good, she lifted a large, flat stone, and crushed it down on the little birds, thus granting them a speedy death instead of a lingering one.[6]

The children were, indeed, excessively nasty, but Anne failed completely in winning either their liking or respect. She was not allowed to punish them, so any threats she made were idle and her pupils were well aware of the fact. Anne's very gentleness merely stimulated them to greater heights of rebellion. When as a last resort, she refused to kiss them goodnight, she was horrified to discover they were completely indifferent to what a Brontë regarded as "the most dreadful of punishments". Eventually Anne was forced to tie her pupils to the legs of the table before she could keep them quiet long enough to mark their lessons.[7] When Mrs Ingham discovered this, Anne was dismissed. She had held her post for scarcely six months, and her humiliation was extreme. Even her family's kindness said, more plainly than words, that she had failed. Yet her failure spurred her on to seek another post. Still eager to make her way in the world, she comforted herself with the reflection that not all children could be as bad as the Inghams.

NOTES TO CHAPTER EIGHT

1. See Charlotte Brontë's Biographical Note on Anne.
2. Anne Brontë, 'Verses by Lady Geralda', written 1836.
3. The Rev. La Trobe described the incident to Mrs Scruton of Thornton, who related it to Mrs Gaskell.
4. See Anne Brontë, *Agnes Grey*.
5. Letter from Charlotte Brontë to Ellen Nussey, 15th April 1839.
6. These incidents, recounted in *Agnes Grey*, were declared by Charlotte to be literal accounts of actual events, underplayed by Anne who feared she might be accused of exaggeration.
7. Mrs Ingham related the incident to one of her grandchildren.

NINE

The Curate

In August 1839, Mr Brontë was given an assistant curate—a fair-haired, blue-eyed young man of twenty-five years, with "classical attainments of the highest order". His name was William Weightman, and he succeeded not only in making the family like him, but in becoming an important member of their close-knit circle.

Part of his secret probably lay in the fact that he expected to be liked. He walked blithely into the quiet Parsonage and won everybody's hearts. Mr Brontë was eventually to regard him as a second son. In Aunt Branwell's eyes, the curate could do no wrong and Charlotte, adopting him as her protégé, was soon advising him about his love affairs. Perhaps, unconsciously, she was attempting to fill the gap left when her collaboration with Branwell faded. Charlotte still loved her brother dearly, but she could no longer close her eyes to the weaknesses in his character. In any event, Branwell was shortly to leave home again.

To Ellen Nussey, Charlotte wrote:

> One thing will make the daily routine more unvaried than ever. Branwell, who used to enliven us, is to leave us in a few days to enter the situation of a private tutor in the neighbourhood of Ulverston. How he will like or settle remains yet to be seen, at present he is full of hope and resolution. I, who know his variable nature, and his strong turn for active life, dare not be too sanguine.[1]

With Branwell settled in his new post William Weightman was the only acceptable male society around. By the spring of 1840 he was already a firm favourite. In February Ellen Nussey came to stay and he promptly began a campaign of sighs, looks and compliments designed to turn that susceptible young lady's head. Charlotte and Ellen, indeed, both lost their heads a little, flirted outrageously, and teased each other about the charming young curate.[2]

What is even more incredible was that Emily, who normally fled from the room if a gentleman were announced, got on famously with William Weightman. She called him, significantly, "Celia Amelia", while he dubbed her the "Sergeant-Major" because she insisted upon acting as chaperone when he took Ellen walking on the moors.[3]

The girls were soon referring to him openly as "Miss Weightman", and he appears to have not only failed to object, but to have persuaded Charlotte to paint his portrait in full academic dress, and to have aroused considerable amusement by his insistence that the texture of the materials should be exactly rendered.[4]

Weightman possessed the gift of pleasing the ladies without becoming personally involved. When he heard that the Brontës had never received Valentines, he walked ten miles in order to post four—the extra one being for Ellen Nussey. This romantic gesture caused intense excitement. It was Mr Weightman also who lectured on the Classics at the Mechanics Institute at Keighley and escorted the girls home at the unheard-of hour of midnight.

It is generally believed that Anne Brontë fell desperately in love with this handsome curate. Certainly her poems seem to suggest this, but how far they are to be taken literally is impossible to tell. Weightman was exactly the kind of agreeable, light-hearted creature to win the heart of a modest, delicate girl. There is no evidence that he reciprocated her interest.[5] Indeed, they were mentioned together only once.

Charlotte wrote to Ellen Nussey:

His "young reverence", as you tenderly call him, is looking delicate and pale, poor thing, don't you pity him? I do, from my heart! When he is well and fat and jovial, I never think of him, but when anything ails him I am always sorry. He sits opposite to Anne in church, sighing softly, and looking out the corners of his eyes to win her attention, and Anne is so quiet, her look so downcast, they are a picture.

While his sisters flirted and gossiped and even fell in love a little, Branwell was at Ulverston, teaching the two sons of Mr Postlethwaite. His duties were light and as he occupied separate lodgings, his evenings were free.

Branwell had turned his attention to writing again, still hoping against hope to break into the literary world. Perhaps his translation of Horace's *Odes* was undertaken as an exercise in mental discipline. Two of these *Odes* and an original poem of his, he despatched to Hartley Coleridge, receiving in return an invitation to visit Ambleside.

Here, in the peace and quiet of the Lake District, lived a man even less equipped to face reality than Branwell. Hartley Coleridge, overshadowed by the more powerful genius of his father, Samuel, had been a child prodigy, having created at the age of six years a dream world called "Ejuxria".

Unhappily, despite his strong literary connections, he could be best described as a brilliant failure. True, he had published a great deal, achieving more success than Branwell dared to attain, but his heavy drinking and violent rages made him at best unreliable, while his abnormal sensitivity made it impossible for him to lead a normal, social existence.[6]

In him, Branwell had discovered a kindred spirit, and the day they spent together in Ambleside was gratefully remembered. Hartley Coleridge encouraged the younger man to continue with his work, whether out of kindness or a realization of Branwell's merit is hard to say. He was, apparently, unsuccessful in his attempts to place any of Branwell's manuscripts, if in fact he ever ventured to submit any to a publisher.[7] Hartley Coleridge doing business on Branwell Brontë's behalf would have been too much like the blind leading the blind.

Nevertheless, even a fleeting contact with an established writer would have been enough to send Branwell's spirits soaring and may have accounted for his suddenly leaving his post. Tradition declares, without proof, that he was dismissed for drunkenness, and that his disgrace was covered by Mr Brontë, who wrote, at Branwell's request, ordering his return. It is far more likely that Branwell persuaded his father that he was at the beginning of a splendid, literary career, and that Mr Brontë obtained his son's release in order that Branwell might devote his entire time to writing.

By the beginning of June 1840, Branwell was back at Haworth, writing steadily, and full of hope for the future. Much of that summer was spent by Branwell in the company of William Weightman. He was a charming, intellectual young man, to whom Branwell was strongly drawn. A great many afternoons were spent shooting together on the moors, and the friendship endured.

But summer cannot last for ever. None of the family was earning money, and Branwell's work was no nearer publication.

By the autumn, Charlotte was writing to Ellen Nussey:

A distant relative of mine, one Patrick Boanerges, has set off to seek his fortune in the wild, wandering, adventurous, romantic, Knight-errant-like capacity of clerk on the Leeds and Manchester Railroad.[3]

The joke did not quite disguise her disappointment. At twenty-three years of age, Branwell had achieved nothing, and his old comrade and fellow collaborator obviously felt only too keenly the humiliation of her brother's position. She was, evidently, the only one in the family to feel like that. Branwell himself was wild with excitement at the prospect of working near the great steam engines now threading their way across the country.

At Sowerby Bridge, Branwell at first made an excellent impression. He suggested several improvements in the organization of the timetable which were adopted by the Railway Committee. Nearby lived the Leyland brothers, with whom Branwell renewed his acquaintanceship. During the long, quiet hours between trains, he could leave the wooden hut where his office was situated, and stroll along to any of the four public houses to enjoy a few drinks.

After six months, he was appointed assistant station master at the branch line of Luddenden Foot, two miles away. His duties were light, but the cheerful bustle of Sowerby was missing. There was very little for him to do, except stare out of the window at the empty tracks or walk along by the canal and chat with the bargees.

There were public houses in the vicinity, and Branwell naturally patronized them. At the Lord Nelson Inn, he could enjoy the company of the railway engineer, Francis Grundy, later to become one of Branwell's most fervent partisans.[9]

The contrast between convivial evenings with Grundy and the loneliness of his workdays was immense. His old failures rose up to mock him, and in a passion of fear he would seize his notebook and write furiously long, laboured verses about brave heroes. His infernal world and the real world struggled for mastery. While his right hand wrote down inventories of freight, his left hand scribbled "Holy Jesu" and "Jesu Salvator". On one occasion, he heard, or thought he heard, the voice of his dead sister, Maria, calling to him above the shunting of the engines.[10] He had moved an infinite distance from the faith of his childhood, and there seemed to be no way back, even if he had wished to make the effort, so he shut his ears to the voice of Maria, and drank a little more deeply.

While Branwell suffered at Luddenden Foot, Charlotte was suffering in Rawdon, near Bradford, where she had taken a second post as governess. Her employers, Mr and Mrs White, were wealthy, respectable, mercantile folk, and Charlotte tried, desperately, to settle down in her new situation.

But, as she wrote to Ellen Nussey :

> . . . no one but myself can tell how hard a governess's work is to me—for no one but myself is aware how utterly averse my whole mind and nature are for the employment. Do not think that I fail to blame myself for this, or that I leave any means unemployed to conquer this feeling. Some of my greatest difficulties lie in things that would appear to you comparatively trivial. I find it so hard to repel the rude familiarity of children. I find it so difficult to ask either servants or mistress for anything I want, however much I want it.[11]

Added to her shyness was perpetual home-sickness. To Henry Nussey, with whom she was still on friendly terms, she wrote :

> My home is humble and unattractive to strangers, but to me it contains what I shall find nowhere else in the world—the profound, the intense affection which brothers and sisters feel for

each other when their minds are cast in the same mould, their ideas drawn from the same source—when they have clung to each other from childhood, and when disputes have never sprung up to divide them.[12]

The thought of spending the rest of her life in a strange household, at the beck and call of unruly pupils and an impatient mistress, was too much to bear. Yet, teaching was the only profession open to her. Slowly a plan formed in her mind, namely, that the Brontës should open their own school. She hinted to Aunt Branwell and to Mr Brontë, but while the elders approved the idea in theory, they pointed out the difficulties. Charlotte had no money or connections, and the sisters possessed no diplomas or certificates that might render their school more attractive to prospective pupils. Meanwhile, Charlotte remained, reluctantly, with the White family and fretted about her younger sister, Anne, now, also, placed in a second situation.

Anne, despite renewed objections from her family, had taken the unusual step of advertising for a post, stating her qualifications and demanding a salary of fifty pounds a year.

The Robinsons of Thorp Green Hall, near York, replied to the advertisement and agreed to her terms, apparently without a personal interview. Her new employer was a clergyman, and this fact probably served to allay Mr Brontë's fears, for Anne was going seventy miles from home.

Anne left Haworth towards the end of March 1841, and travelled all day to her destination. The Robinsons were wealthy, worldly people who led a lively, social life, and were more interested in fox-hunting and balls than in books or the church.

Anne was disillusioned from the outset, for not even the magnificent estates around the Hall could compensate for the loss of that companionship she and Emily had enjoyed during their rambles across the moors.

Written on Emily's anniversary and destined to be opened in four years' time, Anne's "birthday note" betrays her dissatisfaction.

This is Emily's birthday. She has now completed her 23rd year, and is, I believe, at home. Charlotte is a governess in the family of Mr White. Branwell is a clerk in the railroad station at Luddenden Foot, and I am a governess in the family of Mr Robinson. I dislike the situation and wish to change it for another. I am now at Scarborough. My pupils are gone to bed and I am hastening to finish this before I follow them.

We are thinking of setting up a school of our own, but nothing definite is settled about it yet, and we do not know whether we shall be able to or not. I hope we shall.[13]

On the same evening, Emily was also writing a "birthday note", almost identical in content, but very different in tone.

A scheme is at present in agitation for setting up a school of our own; as yet nothing is determined, but I hope and trust it may go on and prosper and answer our highest expectations . . . I guess that at the time appointed for the opening of this paper—We, i.e. Charlotte, Anne and I—shall be merrily seated in our own sittingroom in some pleasant and flourishing seminary, having just gathered in for the midsummer holidays. Our debts will be paid off and we shall have cash in hand to a considerable amount. Papa, Aunt, and Branwell will either have been—or be coming— to visit us. It will be a fine warm summer evening, very different from this bleak look-out. Anne and I will perchance slip out into the garden for a few minutes to peruse our papers. I hope this or something better will be the case.[14]

Emily was well aware as she wrote that Anne would read her paper, and her optimism may have been partly assumed. The sisters were inseparable companions, with an almost tele-pathic bond of sympathy, as the similarity of their birthday notes proves, but they were also Brontës, guarding their privacy.

Emily would look forward to a prosperous future when she wrote for her sister, but, in private, her sentiments were different.

> Riches I hold in light esteem
> And Love I laugh to scorn
> And Lust of Fame was but a dream
> That vanished with the morn—
>
> And if I pray—the only prayer
> That moves my lips for me
> Is "Leave the heart that now I bear
> And give me liberty".

> Yes, as my swift days near their goal
> 'Tis all that I implore—
> Through life and death, a chainless soul
> With courage to endure.[15]

Was this a character from Gondal speaking, or was it the other Emily, unknown to her family, guessed at by biographers, who had loved and had been rejected?

And what is to be made of the poems that Anne was confiding to her notebook?

> O! I am very weary
> Though tears no longer flow;
> My eyes are tired of weeping,
> My heart is sick of woe.
>
> My life is very lonely,
> My days pass heavily,
> I'm weary of repining,
> Wilt thou not come to me?
>
> Oh, didst thou know my longings
> For thee, from day to day,
> My hopes, so often blighted,
> Thou wouldst not thus delay.[16]

Was this, too, an exile from Gondal, or were these Anne's own feelings as the bud of her romance with William Weightman failed to bloom?

While the younger sisters wrote their yearning poems, Charlotte was busy translating dreams into action. The Taylors were at a finishing school in Brussels, and Mary Taylor wrote such a glowing account of the beauties of the city that Charlotte was filled with a burning desire to travel. The thought of seeing the great cathedrals, the paintings and statues, of which she had only read, brought "such a vehement impatience of restraint and steady work; such a strong wish for wings—wings such as wealth can furnish, such an earnest thirst to see, to know, to learn, something internal seemed to expand boldly for a minute".[17]

There was one way in which Charlotte could attain her ambition. If they wished to open a school, they would stand a better chance of success if they first spent some time on the

Continent, perfecting that veneer of sophistication that travel abroad imparts.

Miss Wooler on the verge of retirement, had offered them her school at Dewsbury, but Charlotte knew that she would have no peace if she remained calmly in England. She wrote to Aunt Branwell, begging her to lend enough money to enable two of them to study for six months in Belgium.

> Papa will perhaps think it is a wild, and ambitious scheme, but who ever rose in the world without ambitions? When he left Ireland to go to Cambridge University, he was as ambitious as I am now. I want us *all* to get on. I know we have talents, and I want them to be turned to account. I look to you, aunt, to help us. I think you will not refuse. I know, if you consent, it shall not be my fault if you ever repent your kindness.[18]

Aunt Branwell agreed to lend Charlotte and Emily sufficient money to enable them to live in Brussels for several months, and suddenly Charlotte's narrow little world had expanded to an immeasurable distance, and her enthusiasm caught up the rest of the family and swept them along in her wake.

NOTES TO CHAPTER NINE

1. Letter from Charlotte Brontë to Ellen Nussey, 28th December 1839.
2. Letter from Charlotte Brontë to Ellen Nussey.
3. Reminiscence of Ellen Nussey.
4. Letter from Charlotte Brontë to Ellen Nussey, 1841.
5. A poem in *Agnes Grey* by Anne Brontë beginning with the line "Oh, they have robbed me of the hope" seems to suggest that her family had counselled her against taking Weightman's attentions too seriously.
6. Margaret Lane, *The Brontë Story*, page 100.
7. Letter from Branwell Brontë to Hartley Coleridge.
8. Letter from Charlotte Brontë to Ellen Nussey.
9. Grundy was wildly inaccurate in remembering dates but possessed great insight into character and divined more than any other outsider the genuine sweetness of Branwell's character.
10. Charlotte used the incident in *Jane Eyre*, and later assured

Mrs Gaskell that it was absolutely true. Branwell recounted
the event in his poem, 'Remember Me'.
11. Letter from Charlotte Brontë to Ellen Nussey.
12. Letter from Charlotte Brontë to Henry Nussey.
13. Birthday Note by Anne Brontë, 30th July 1840.
14. Birthday Note by Emily Brontë, 30th July 1840.
15. Emily Brontë, 'The Old Stoic', 1st March 1841.
16. Anne Brontë, 'Appeal', 28th August 1841.
17. Letter from Charlotte Brontë to Ellen Nussey, 7th August 1841.
18. Letter from Charlotte Brontë to Miss Branwell, 29th September 1841.

TEN

Brussels

Events moved with surprising swiftness. Charlotte had decided that Emily should accompany her to Brussels, and, by some miracle, Emily had agreed to go. Anne had had no success in finding another post, so after Christmas, returned to Thorp Green. Duty alone must have dictated her actions, for she was unhappy in her situation; but fifty pounds a year was an excellent salary for a governess—thirty pounds more than Charlotte had earned with the White family.

In February 1842, Mr Brontë and the Taylors escorted Charlotte and Emily to Brussels, to the Pensionnat Heger, Rue d'Isabelle. They broke their journey in London, staying for several days at the Chapter Coffee House in Paternoster Row, where, according to Mary Taylor, "Charlotte seemed to think our business was, and ought to be, to see all the pictures and statues we could".[1]

The Pensionnat Heger was a large, seventeenth-century building housing more than a hundred pupils. Monsieur and Madame Heger conducted the establishment in a business-like and decorous way. Madame was a neat, plump, pleasantly spoken woman with several children. Monsieur, also in his mid-thirties, was small, fiery and sallow-complexioned, with a considerable amount of Gallic charm and a gift for teaching which amounted almost to genius.

Charlotte at twenty-six years of age, and Emily at twenty-four, were the eldest pupils in the school. They were also the only British inmates and the only Protestants—three circumstances which would have set them apart, even if their singular appearance had not.

According to Mrs Gaskell:

> The two sisters clung together, and kept apart from the herd of happy, boisterous, well-befriended Belgian girls, who, in their turn, thought the new, English pupils wild and scared-looking, with strange, odd, insular ideas about dress; for Emily had taken a fancy to the fashion, ugly and preposterous even during its reign, of gigot sleeves, and persisted in wearing them long after they were 'gone out'. Her petticoats, too, had not a curve or a wave in them, but hung down straight and long clinging to her lank figure.[2]

The Brontës, held back by shyness and distaste, kept themselves aloof from the other pupils and mistresses. They studied together in class, slept in twin beds at the end of the main dormitory, and walked together at recreation time, up and down the pleached alleys. Emily, the taller, always leaned upon Charlotte's shoulder and if anybody addressed them, Charlotte did the talking for both.

Monsieur Heger was impressed by their studious ways and high intelligence, and gave them private lessons in French. He quickly sensed the extreme femininity beneath Charlotte's plain exterior and found that he could obtain better work by flattering her a little and teasing her out of her shyness. Emily was a different proposition. Not only was she insensible to flattery, but she did not scruple to argue fiercely when she considered Heger's teaching methods to be ill-advised.[3]

Nevertheless, the Brontës made great strides in their knowledge of French, and even began to do some teaching themselves. Although the fees at the Pensionnat were modest, the loan from Aunt Branwell had to be carefully husbanded, and the Hegers may have tactfully discovered a way in which the girls could earn pocket-money.

Occasionally they went sight-seeing with the Taylor girls, or accepted an invitation to tea from Mrs Letitia Wheelwright, an English lady living in Brussels. These social engagements, modest as they were, were endured rather than enjoyed. Emily never opened her mouth except to say "Goodbye", and Charlotte, even when drawn into conversation, would gradually twist round in her chair until her face was hidden from her listeners.[4]

They were not, however, apparently quite as homesick as later biographers have maintained. Charlotte enjoyed the novelty of being a pupil again, and undoubtedly appreciated the fine architecture abounding in the city, even if the evidence of Catholicism everywhere disgusted her militant Protestantism.*

Mary Taylor wrote home to Ellen Nussey :

> Charlotte and Emily are well not only in health but in mind and hope. They are content with their present position and even gay.[5]

At home, there was little contentment and gaiety. Two months after Charlotte and Emily left for Brussels, Branwell was dismissed from his job at Luddenden Foot. When the auditors came down at the end of the financial year, they discovered a deficit of eleven pounds odd, for which Branwell was unable to account; which is not surprising, because his ledgers were full of drawings and broken phrases of verse. It was discovered that he had been in the habit of drinking all day while the porter looked after the ticket office, and helped himself to the contents of the till.

Branwell was disgraced, and arrived home in a state of near-collapse. The real world had broken into his infernal world. The Earl of Northangerland could not even hold down a clerical post for more than a few months. Now, when it was too late, he tried desperately to be reinstated on the Railway, but it was useless, and even Grundy was unable to give his friend any practical advice.[6]

The solitary ray of sunshine lay in the publication of some of Branwell's poems in the *Halifax Guardian* and *Leeds Intelligencer*. Signed by the pseudonym, 'Northangerland', they represented slight literary success, but while their publication lifted Branwell out of his abyss of depression, even Branwell could not rebuild his hopes of becoming a major poet. The poems themselves display, clearly, Branwell's own state of mind.

* Charlotte declared that if anybody were so besotted as to wish to turn Catholic after attending Mass, then she wished them luck.

Why dost thou sorrow for the happy dead?
For if their life be lost, their toils are o'er
And woe and want shall trouble them no more,
Nor ever slept they in an earthly bed
So sound as now they sleep while, dreamless laid
In the dark chambers of that unknown shore
Where Night and Silence seal each guarded door.
So, turn from such as these thy drooping head
And mourn the 'Dead Alive' whose spirit flies—
Whose life departs before his death has come—
Who finds no Heaven beyond Life's gloomy skies.
Who sees no Hope to brighten up that gloom,
'Tis HE who feels the warm that never dies—
The REAL death and the darkness of the tomb.[7]

Branwell appears to have been fated throughout his life to lose the very people who might have instilled in him hope and resolution. The deaths of Maria and Elizabeth had shocked the eight-year-old boy into an awareness of death before he was even aware of the nature of life.

His close friendship with William Weightman was destined also to end. That Branwell felt an almost physical attraction to the curate is evident from the lines he wrote, in which Weightman's nickname 'Amelia' is openly used.

When you, Amelia, feel like me
The dullness of satiety,
You will not smile as now you smile,
With lips that even me beguile.[8]

Unhappily, the beguiling curate fell ill and died suddenly. The cause of death was given as "cholera and peritonitis", a conveniently vague term which covered almost any illness arising from the summer heat. Branwell apparently nursed his friend during his last hours and was so grief-stricken by his death that he actually consented to attend the funeral service, sobbing loudly throughout the sermon.*

William Weightman, despite his faults, had brought gaiety to the Brontës. Never again would a strange young man be admitted so readily into their circle. Upon Anne, the blow fell the heaviest and was all the more intolerable because she had nobody with whom to share her sorrow. Charlotte and Emily

* The villagers were, apparently, very surprised to see him in church at all.

mourned a friend, but from Anne's poems, written later, it seems clear that she mourned more than that.

> Cold in the grave for years has lain
> The form it was my bliss to see;
> And only dreams can bring again
> The darling of my heart to me.[9]

Charlotte and Emily had scarcely received tidings of Weightman's death, when Mary Taylor's younger sister, Martha, died suddenly. The Taylor sisters were staying in the suburb of Knockelburg, from whence they could easily drive over to the Heger Pensionnat.

Martha was scarcely twenty-three years old, described by Ellen Nussey as "not in the least pretty, but something much better, full of change and variety, rudely outspoken, lively and original, producing laughter with her own good humour and affection".[10]

Charlotte declared that Martha had died of the same cause as William Weightman. Mrs Gaskell used the familiar term "low fever". The death certificate gave no cause of death and was not signed by any doctor. Martha died at ten p.m. on 10th October 1842, and "two Belgian gentlemen" reported the fact some four hours later. She was buried at once in the Protestant cemetery, in a manner that suggests unusual haste.

Significantly, the Brontës made no further reference to her death, and the usually forthright Mary wrote cryptically to Ellen Nussey.

> You will wish to hear the history of Martha's illness—I will give you it in a few months; till then you must excuse me. A thousand times I have reviewed the minutest circumstances of it, but I cannot without great difficulty give a regular account of them. There is nothing to regret, nothing to recall—not even Martha. She is better where she is. But when I recall the sufferings that have purified her, my heart aches—but I can't help it, and every trivial accident, sad or gay, reminds me of her.[11]

If Martha had, indeed, perished of a "low fever", there should have been great regret at her untimely end, and, if she did die in such a fever, then surely the practical Mary would have summoned a doctor. One would also give much to know the identity of the "two Belgian gentlemen" who reported her death. Later, Emily was to base much of the character of Catherine Earnshaw upon the character of Martha Taylor, and Cathy's death in childbirth possibly paralleled reality.

Charlotte and Emily were still buying mourning clothes for Weightman and Martha, when an urgent message arrived from home to tell them Aunt Branwell was seriously ill. Duty demanded their immediate return, but, for Charlotte at least, the summons cannot have brought any relief. She had largely conquered her home-sickness, and enjoyed the delightful, if dangerous, privilege of being Monsieur Heger's favourite pupil.

The sisters arrived too late to be of any practical help.

On 29th October, Branwell wrote to his friend, Grundy:

I am incoherent, I fear, but I have been waking two nights witnessing such agonizing suffering as I would not wish my worst enemy to endure; and I have now lost the guide and director of all the happy days connected with my childhood.

The cause of Aunt Branwell's death was "exhaustion from constipation"—a condition easily remedied these days, but incurable in 1842. Branwell has been accused of hypocrisy in his grief, but it was perfectly in character that he, alone of the family, should grieve for the irritable, pious, exacting little Cornishwoman, who had lived her last twenty years in an alien land. Branwell had thrown away her teachings, but his gratitude for her generosity had never died. He had remained the favoured nephew, the brilliant boy, and her death severed another link with that security of his early childhood.

Anne had asked Mrs Robinson for leave to go home to nurse her aunt, but permission came so slowly that she arrived only shortly before her sisters. None of them was particularly upset by their aunt's decease. Indeed, Charlotte wrote to Ellen Nussey, urging her not to delay a proposed visit.

Do not fear to find us melancholy or depressed. We are much as usual. You will see no difference from our former demeanour.[12]

There was, however, a distinct difference in their finances; Aunt Branwell, in a will drawn up nine years earlier, had divided her money between her Brontë nieces and a Cornish niece. They were now the richer by some two or three hundred pounds each. Their aunt had also divided her possessions among them, and left to Branwell her "Japan dressing box"—not because his behaviour had disappointed her,[13] for the will had been made when Branwell's future was still brightly shining. She evidently considered that Branwell would make his own way in the world. It was the girls who would need financial protection.

There was now no obstacle to their setting up a school, but the project hung fire. Charlotte had convinced herself that a further year in Brussels would better her education. The Hegers offered free bed and board in return for her teaching services.[14] Emily was also asked to return, but flatly refused. Tabby was now very lame and John Brown's little daughter, Martha, could not, at fourteen, be expected to do all the heavy work.

Emily, with her tireless energy, was ideally suited for the tasks which, thanks to her early training, she could perform efficiently, even while her mind wandered far away in Gondal.

Anne must return to Thorp Green Hall, but she would not be returning alone. Branwell had obtained a post there as tutor to the Robinsons' eleven-year-old son, Edmund. Anne, aware of Branwell's need for employment, had probably recommended her brother for the position. Although she considered her employers too worldly, she must have thought that Branwell would enjoy their society, and perhaps she, too, craved a familiar face.

Anne and Branwell left home together in mid-January 1843, and on the 27th of that month, Charlotte returned to Brussels.

Emily alone remained as housekeeper to her father. The solitary life suited her peculiar nature. Although she personally was described as "tall and ungainly, always looking untidy",[15] the Parsonage was spotless and Emily was often seen kneading bread in the kitchen, with the door open and a book propped on the shelf before her.

Emily had moved into the little study-bedroom where Maria and Elizabeth had once slept and it is fairly certain that, in this bedroom, she conducted her experiments in those realms of the unconscious, which she described so exquisitely in her poems.

> I'm happiest when most away
> I can bear my soul from its home of clay
> On a windy night when the moon is bright
> And the eye can wander through worlds of light.

When I am not and none beside—
Nor earth nor sea nor cloudless sky—
But only spirit wandering wide
Through infinite immensity.[16]

With ideas such as these, it is not surprising that Emily, like the others, had no notion of the real motive for Charlotte's return to Brussels—a motive Charlotte herself refused to recognize.

NOTES TO CHAPTER TEN

1. Statement to Mrs Gaskell by Mary Taylor.
2. Mrs Gaskell, *Life of Charlotte Brontë.*
3. Charlotte in a letter to Ellen Nussey declared that "Emily and Monsier Heger do not draw together well at all".
4. Both the Wheelwrights and their friend, Mrs Jenkins, remembered this extreme shyness.
5. Letter from Mary Taylor to Ellen Nussey.
6. A letter in which Branwell Brontë begged Grundy to use his influence on his behalf is still in existence.
7 Branwell Brontë, 'Peaceful Death and Painful Life'; this poem appeared in the *Halifax Guardian* on 14th May 1842.
8. Poem by Branwell Brontë.
9. Poem by Anne Brontë, written 1845.
10. Statement by Ellen Nussey to Mrs Gaskell.
11. Letter from Mary Taylor to Ellen Nussey.
12. Letter from Charlotte Brontë to Ellen Nussey.
13. Mrs Gaskell, evidently not examining the date on the document, declared that Miss Branwell had cut out her nephew.
14. Letter from Monsieur Heger to Mr Brontë.
15. Statement by Mrs Wheelwright.
16. Poem by Emily Brontë (undated).

ELEVEN

Monsieur Heger

Charlotte had persuaded herself that her thirst for education sent her away from home, but her admiration for Monsieur Heger, as a teacher, had now become an obsession for the man himself. She constantly under-rated him, telling Ellen Nussey that he was "a little, black, ugly being something between an insane tomcat, and a delirious hyena".[1]

She travelled alone to London, intending to stay overnight at the Chapter Coffee House, but the train was delayed and it was ten o'clock at night when she arrived. Too shy to check in at an hotel so late at night, she preferred to go directly to the Ostend packet boat. Apparently unaware that passengers were not allowed to sleep on board, she explained her predicament to the Captain, who waived the rules and permitted her to occupy a berth.[2] An odd shyness, surely, that prevents a lady from going to an hotel at night, but allows her to hire a boatman and be rowed out to a strange ship requesting permission to board!

At first, she was welcomed as an old friend of the Hegers, who invited her to share their sitting-room when lessons were done. It was a privilege of which Charlotte, fearing to intrude, seldom availed herself.[3]

Charlotte taught English to a large section of the Belgian pupils and established order in her class, if we are to believe *Villette*, by the simple expedient of pushing the ringleader into a cupboard and locking the door. She studied German with Monsieur Heger and, in return, tried to instruct him in English pronunciation. It should have been a time of reasonable contentment, but it was to prove a time of anguish, as Charlotte slowly realized the true nature of her feelings and even tardily apprehended that the Hegers were also conscious of her infatuation.

It was an infatuation that filled her loneliness. There was now no Emily with whom to walk at recreation time, and no Taylor sisters with whom to go sightseeing. Martha lay in the cemetery at Knockelburg, and Mary was studying in Germany.

To Branwell, Charlotte confessed.

It is a curious, metaphysical fact that always in the evening when I am in the great dormitory alone, having no other company than a number of beds with white curtains, I always recur as fanatically as ever to the old ideas, the old faces, and the old scenes in the world below.[4]

The infernal world had seized her again, and, to the accusations of her conscience, was added a fresh torment. She was not merely living out her sexual desires with a faceless Zamorna. She was transferring those desires to the Belgian professor, whom she now designated "the black swan".

Charlotte may have imagined that her feelings were hidden. She could not ignore the gradual withdrawal of her employers' friendship, however. Heger began to avoid her, while Madame behaved with noticeable coolness. She began to snub Charlotte, to deliberately exclude her from conversations, and to contrive to be present whenever her husband and Charlotte were together.[5] Charlotte even began to suspect that Madame Heger searched her drawers and bureau in the hope of finding incriminating letters and papers.

One wonders what Madame would have made of the entry, scribbled by Charlotte in her school Atlas.

I am very cold—there is no fire—I wish I were at home with Papa, Branwell, Emily, Anne and Tabby—I am tired of being among foreigners—it is a dreary life—especially as there is only one person in this house worthy of being liked—also another, who seems a rosy sugar plum but I know her to be coloured chalk.

During the long summer vacation, the Hegers went on holiday to the seaside, leaving Charlotte alone at the Pensionnat. She exhausted herself by long walks about the city, returning at night to the great, white-shrouded furniture. She suffered, at this time, from nightmares, and from insomnia also. Something apart from her love for Heger appears to have troubled her—possibly a renewed attack of religious melancholy. She lived through "a nameless experience, that had the hue, the mien, the terror, the very tone of a visitation from eternity".

In a state of mind bordering on insanity, Charlotte did what she would never, at any other time, have contemplated. She went into a Catholic church and confessed to a priest. What she confessed has never been known. She told Emily that the priest allowed her to make a confession, even though she told him she was a Protestant, but she never wrote down the nature of her revelations and it is doubtful if Emily, intensely secretive herself, ever enquired.

The curious episode was never again to be repeated. Neither does Charlotte's confession seem to have brought her any relief.[6]

When school reassembled, Charlotte struggled on, burdened not only by conscience and frustration, but by the added humiliation of knowing that the Hegers were tired of her excessive emotionalism. Finally, she gave in her notice. Significantly, although Madame Heger was more than willing to bid her good-bye, Monsieur flew into a passion and made Charlotte promise to remain a while longer.

To Ellen Nussey, Charlotte wrote:

> I have much to say, many little odd things queer and puzzling enough, which I do not like to trust to a letter, but which one day perhaps or rather one evening, if ever we should find ourselves again at the fireside at Haworth, or at Brookroyd with our feet on the fender, curling our hair, I may communicate to you.[7]

If Heger had indeed flirted with the prim little English spinster, even Charlotte could not imagine that his interest was serious. But she obviously attempted to arouse his love, and Heger evidently flattered and teased her, being completely unaware of the hysteria beneath her demure façade, until his clear-sighted wife informed him.

In December 1843 Charlotte eventually found the courage to leave the object of her devotion. It must, indeed, have required supreme bravery, for Heger had become an obsession. Yet she was fully aware that a conflict between her love and her repressive conscience might end in complete mental break-down.

Even so, she could not resist begging Heger to write to her and Madame Heger was by now so openly hostile that she insisted upon being present when Charlotte said her farewell to Heger. It was an act for which Charlotte never forgave Madame Heger.

Love for Heger was to continue to fill her mind and heart. Charlotte dare not confide in anybody at home, but her letters to Brussels continued to bombard him.

> Day and night I find neither rest nor peace. If I sleep I am disturbed by tormenting dreams in which I see you, always severe, always grave, always incensed against me. Forgive me, then, Monsieur, if I adopt the course of writing to you again? How can I endure life if I make no effort to ease its sufferings?[8]

Again Charlotte wrote:

> To forbid me to write to you, to refuse to answer me, would be to tear from me my last joy on earth, to deprive me of my last privilege.[9]

On the back of the letter, Heger scribbled a reminder to fetch his boots from the cobblers. None of his letters to Char-lotte has survived, although he admitted to Mrs Gaskell that he did in fact answer her and was so anxious that she should find them that it appears obvious that Heger, at least, had had no desire to prolong the embarrassing affair. Even so, Madame Heger, according to her daughter, retrieved Charlotte's torn-up letters from the wastepaper basket where her husband had thrown them, pasted them together and hid them in her jewel case. Whether she intended to use them as a weapon against Charlotte, or against her husband, is not known.[10]

Charlotte informed nobody at home of her feelings, but they had already altered the course of her life. She had begun by inventing a mythical lover, then had transferred the attributes of this phantom to a living man. Not until she had presented the real man under the guise of fiction, would her outraged conscience be appeased, and the flame of her passion die down to ashes.

> He saw my heart's woe, discovered my soul's anguish,
> How in fever, in thirst, in atrophy it pined;
> Knew it could heal, yet looked and let it languish
> To its moans spirit-deaf, to its pangs spirit-blind.
> But once a year he heard a whisper low and dreary
> Appealing for aid, entreating some reply;
> Only when sick, soul-worn, and torture weary,
> Breathed I that prayer, heaved I that sigh.
> He was mute as is the grave, he stood stirless as a tower;
> At last I looked up, and saw I prayed to stone,
> I asked help of that which to help had no power,
> I sought love where love was utterly unknown.[11]

Inevitably Charlotte's feelings were agonized by remorse so deep that she literally feared damnation. But just as Anne had succeeded in abandoning Calvanistic tenets, so Charlotte could finally write:

> He gave our hearts to love; He will not love despise,
> E'en if the gift be lost, as mine was long ago;
> He will forgive the fault, will bid the offender rise,
> Wash out with dews of bliss the fiery brand of woe.

Meanwhile, there was still one hope—a means whereby Charlotte could occupy her days, and keep some control over her mind. The school project, so long delayed, was discussed continually throughout 1844.

The site of the school had never really been settled. The sisters had considered various places, but Mr Brontë's sight was beginning to fail. None of them felt like leaving him and, for Emily in particular, the idea of converting the Parsonage into a school was an attractive one. It is not clear where the boarders were expected to sleep, but there was some talk of extensions to the house.

The circular, printed and distributed, was a businesslike document, offering a boarding-school education to a "limited number of Young Ladies" for an annual fee of thirty-five pounds. French, German, Latin, Music and Drawing would be considered as extras, for a quarterly fee of one guinea each.

There was only one drawback. Not a single pupil appeared. Nobody had heard of the Misses Brontë, and nobody wished to send their daughters to an obscure village high in the bleak North. Although the Nusseys and the Taylors worked indefatigably, sending out copies of the Prospectus to their friends and acquaintances, the school remained a miasma. The project talked about, and worked for, during two years, vanished like a puff of smoke.

Anne left the Robinsons in June 1845. By then, the school plan had failed, so she could not have returned in the hope of aiding her sisters. Branwell was still in his post and apparently took no interest in the school scheme.

Charlotte seized the opportunity to visit Ellen Nussey when, perhaps, they curled their hair and exchanged the promised confidences. Mary Taylor, true to her nature, had taken the revolutionary step of emigrating to New Zealand, where she remained for fifteen years. Letters continued to pass between her and Charlotte, and with a safe distance between, it is likely that Charlotte confided in Mary far more than Ellen.

On 30th June, Emily and Anne visited York, travelling alone together for the first time. Anne had previously visited York with the Robinsons, and probably wished to show Emily the Minster, but Emily has left no record of her impressions of the building that aroused in Anne such high aesthetic appreciation.

Charlotte returned from her visit to Brookroyd on 19th July, and was soon writing to Ellen.

It was ten-o-clock at night when I got home. I found Branwell ill. He is so often owing to his own fault. I was not therefore greatly shocked at first, but when Anne informed me of the immediate cause of his present illness, I was greatly shocked. He had last Thursday received a note from Mr Robinson, sternly dismissing him, intimating that he had discovered his proceedings, which he characterized as bad beyond expression, and charging him on pain of exposure to break off instantly and for ever all communication with every member of his family. We have had sad work with Branwell since. He thought of nothing but stunning or drowning his distress of mind. No one in the house could have rest.[12]

The reason for Branwell's dismissal was confessed by him to have been a love affair with his employer's wife. The Thorp Green affair was then no theoretical problem, but a shameful humiliation for the entire family. For any family it would have been a painful scandal—for the proud, reserved Brontës, it was a blow from which none of them entirely recovered.

NOTES TO CHAPTER ELEVEN

1. Letter from Charlotte Brontë to Ellen Nussey.
2. See Mrs Gaskell's *Life of Charlotte Brontë*.
3. Letter from Charlotte Brontë to Ellen Nussey.
4. Letter from Charlotte Brontë to Branwell Brontë, 1st May 1843.
5. Mrs Gaskell accounted for this by declaring that Charlotte's religious bigotry cause friction between the two women. She had, however, seen Charlotte's letters to Heger, but decided not to use them.
6. These experiences were described by Charlotte in *Villette*.
7. Letter from Charlotte Brontë to Ellen Nussey, December 1843.
8. Letter from Charlotte Brontë to Monsieur Heger.
9. Letter from Charlotte Brontë to Monsieur Heger.
10. Monsieur Heger's daughter Louise presented the letters—four in number—to the British Museum in 1913.
11. Poem by Charlotte Brontë (undated).
12. Letter from Charlotte Brontë to Ellen Nussey, 1845.

TWELVE

Thorp Green

It is extremely doubtful now if the truth about the Thorp Green episode will ever be known. According to the version given by Branwell, and repeated to Mrs Gaskell by Mr Brontë, Lydia Robinson had fallen desperately in love with her son's tutor. When her husband discovered what was happening, Branwell was dismissed. The story sounds simple enough, and yet, all through the history of Branwell's two-and-a-half years at Thorp Green, odd questions arise, to tease the imagination, and to cast doubts on the validity of the story.

To begin with, although Branwell claimed to have written to, and received, love-letters from Lydia Robinson—not one of these interesting documents has survived. Either they were destroyed or they never existed. All our knowledge of the affair comes from Branwell's own statements and letters to his friends, in which he described Mrs Robinson as pining away for love of him. If Mrs Robinson were pining, she concealed her feelings admirably. The Robinsons' social diary remained as full as ever, and her own daughters, in writing to Anne, mentioned their mother's high spirits.

When Mrs Gaskell wrote in her biography of Charlotte, "the woman goes flaunting about to this day in respectable society, a showy woman for her age; kept afloat by her reputed wealth. I see her name in county papers, as one of those who patronize the Christmas balls, and I hear of her in London drawing-rooms. Now let us read, not merely of the sufferings of her guilty accomplice, but of the misery she caused to innocent victims, whose premature deaths may, in part, be laid at her door", she was immediately threatened with a libel suit. It might have been a bluff or an attempt to vindicate Mrs Robinson's reputation, but her publisher eventually removed the offending passage. The Robinsons declared themselves eager to go to law, but finally agreed upon a settlement out of court.

Those who support the love affair theory, cite the internal evidence of Anne Brontë's poems and diary papers, which point quite clearly to having suffered great anxiety of spirit when she and Branwell were at Thorp Green. Her sparse comments can, however, be interpreted quite differently.

In the beginning, Anne disliked her position and wished to change it for another.[1] This has been taken to mean that she saw from the beginning the depraved character of her employers. But, even with a salary of fifty pounds a year, she would scarcely have remained in an openly dissolute household, far less brought her impressionable brother there.

Anne had been for two years at Thorp Green when she recommended her brother as tutor. She had reconciled herself to her position, and had gained the affection of her pupils. They took her with them on excursions to York, and to Scarborough; and they bought her a spaniel puppy, called Flossy.

Anne's uneasiness grew upon her *after* she had introduced Branwell into the Robinson circle. At first, all seemed well. Mr Brontë visited Thorp Green, and told Charlotte that both Anne and Branwell were "wondrously valued in their situations".[2]

Branwell's pupil, Edmund, was about eleven years old when the tutor was engaged. Branwell lodged, not in the main Hall, but in the dower-house within the grounds, where Edmund attended daily for his lessons. The building was called 'Monk's House', and was, apparently, part of the original monastery on the site of which Thorp Green was built. In the evenings Branwell was sometimes invited to sit with the family, but they could scarcely have invited the tutor without asking the governess too. Branwell can hardly have conducted a passionate love affair with his sister sewing quietly in the corner.

Yet, according to later gossip, Branwell and Mrs Robinson

actually made love in front of her children, who would then threaten to tell their father unless she gave them money.[3] The story seems incredible, especially when the character of the alleged lover is recalled. Branwell, who shied away when he suspected Mary Taylor of falling in love with him, could never have acted in so blatant and shameless a fashion.

Indeed, in the absence of proven facts, it is from the characters of the people concerned that one may obtain the most accurate impression of what really happened.

Lydia Robinson was seventeen years older than Branwell, and was described as handsome and elegant. She possessed a comfortable fortune in her own right, was an active supporter of many charities, and subscribed to several libraries.[4]

Branwell writing of his love to Grundy gave his friend to understand that Mr Robinson treated his wife cruelly.[5] The Thorp Green account books suggest otherwise. Mr Robinson evidently showered gifts of books, jewellery, and clothes upon her, throughout their married life. It is obvious that his affection was returned. In the account book, 1846, shortly after Mr Robinson' death, the words "my angel Edmund" appear in her handwriting opposite various items of expense connected with the funeral.[6]

If Lydia Robinson did show any interest in Branwell, it was possibly a motherly one. Branwell was young, attractive, and he wrote poetry. Mrs Robinson, like any woman verging on middle age, would enjoy the flattery of a sparkling youth, but that she would have thrown overboard her principles, risk her social position, and lay herself open to blackmail, is almost inconceivable. Such things have, of course, happened. But Mrs Robinson, judging by the affection she showered on her family, had a strong maternal streak.

However, Branwell was certainly dismissed, if not for the reason he gave. The circumstances of his dismissal, and the events leading up to it, are themselves very curious.

During Branwell's period of employment at Thorp Green, Anne was suffering deeply. It has been assumed, too readily, that she was the unwilling witness of a sordid affair between Mrs Robinson and her brother. Her poems suggest that she had even remonstrated with Branwell and been snubbed for her pains.

Grieving to look on vice and sin,
Yet powerless to quell
The silent current from within,
The outward torrent's swell;
While all the good I would impart,
The feelings I would share,
Are driven backwards to my heart,
And turned to wormwood there.[7]

Anne wrote nothing of the details of the affair. Indeed, she referred to it only twice, and then indirectly. On the back of her Prayer Book, she wrote: "Sick of mankind and their disgusting ways." Was it a brief summary of a particular sermon, or did Anne's feelings suddenly overwhelm her when she had no other paper to hand?[8]

In the diary paper, written after her return from Thorp Green, occurs the sentence: "During my stay I have had some very unpleasant and undreamt of experiences of human nature."[9]

The phrase is a curious one. Anne was innocent, but she was not ignorant. She would have been shocked to discover that her brother was having an affair but it would not have been an "undreamt of experience". Anne had already written a great deal about Gondal, and the arch-heroine of her secret world was, to say the least, generous with her favours.

Then, the letter in which Mr Robinson dismissed Branwell, used expressions that appear excessively strong, even for adultery: "proceedings bad beyond expression", and "charging him on pain of exposure to break off instantly and forever all communication with every member of his family".[10]

To expose Branwell would have been to expose his wife too, yet the Robinsons remained devoted to each other, and Mr Robinson made no attempt to alter his will in order to punish his wife for infidelity. Even if Lydia was innocent and Branwell had been forcing his attentions on her, Mr Robinson would surely have specified this in his letter, which was actually addressed, not to Branwell, but to Mr Brontë.

That Mr Robinson was furiously angry is quite clear, but his words are guarded. Presumably he wished to spare the feelings of his fellow clergyman and therefore did not specify the exact nature of Branwell's crime. Was this because the crime itself might have been one that to Mr Brontë would appear even more horrible than adultery?

Anne Marshall, Mrs Robinson's personal maid, may have known the full story. The account books reveal that she was being paid twelve pounds per annum. Certain promissory notes, amounting to more than five hundred pounds, were made out to her after Mr Robinson's death by his widow, which seems to indicate quite clearly that both Branwell's employers used Anne Marshall in a capacity other than that of lady's maid. They may have been paying her to spy on their son's tutor, but such large sums of money appear excessive for merely spying. Were they also designed to keep Anne Marshall silent about what she discovered?

Branwell was actually dismissed in his absence. The Robinsons went to Scarborough for their usual holiday on 4th July 1845. Edmund did not join his parents until 17th July.[11] On that very day, Mr Robinson wrote the letter of dismissal. Branwell had been alone with Edmund for over a week. One wonders what the thirteen-year-old boy said to his parents that caused Mr Robinson to act with such haste. One would also like to know why Dr Thorpe, the family physician, was immediately called in to question him. More than two years later, Mrs Robinson wrote to her lawyer:

> I hope Dr T may be less unguarded in questioning Edmund than he used to be . . . for I am well aware of the things he has said to me concerning Thorp Green and *all* which had better not have been said. And I am *very* glad you talked to my son upon it by naming 'him' in Dr Thorpe's presence.

Having been thoroughly cross-examined, thirteen-year-old Edmund was packed off to Somerset in charge of a neighbouring clergyman and he remained away from home for more than four years, though his sisters remained at home.

To suggest that Branwell was actually homosexual would be to build an over-simplified case on flimsy evidence. That Branwell had a feminine streak in his character is fairly certain. Apart from his poems, written often from a female point of view, there was his close kinship with the vaguely effeminate Weightman and his panic when a light flirtation with Mary Taylor threatened to turn to something more serious. Then

G

there is curious internal evidence in a story written by Charlotte, while in her teens, in which she addresses her brother as a "wry-faced hermaphrodite".[12]

If Branwell had, in fact, attempted to corrupt his pupil, he would never have dared to confess the fact to his family. Instead, numbed with shock at the disgrace, he could only stammer of his passion for Mrs Robinson, and having invented the love affair, believe in it more fervently than anybody.

It is impossible to tell whether or not his family believed him. Charlotte's letters to Ellen Nussey speak most bitterly of Mrs Robinson, but they are no guarantee of the truth of Branwell's story. In the Victorian age, sodomy was not an illness but a vice so dreadful that it was scarcely recognized, let alone mentioned, in polite society. Charlotte, in her letters, never confided fully in Ellen about her own affairs, so that it is unlikely that she would ever reveal such a terrible facet of her adored brother's nature.

Charlotte's disillusionment with the companion of her early years was complete. Chief Genius Brannii was dead. She had nothing in common with the shambling, drug-ridden, drunkard, who veered between tearful repentance and threats to cut his sisters' throats and blow out his brains. She refused to speak to him and told Ellen Nussey that it was impossible to remain in the room when he was there.[13]

At the very same time, Charlotte was writing to Heger. Her position, although innocent, was comparable to her brother's. If Branwell had genuinely loved Mrs Robinson, then Charlotte would surely have grieved for him, even if she did not condone his actions. She knew only too well the pangs of unrequited love. But Charlotte, neither in words nor deeds, expressed sympathy or grief. Her attitude was one of cold contempt.

Anne, apart from her brief entries in private papers, remained silent on the subject. She, of all the family, was in a position to know the truth, but she said nothing. Only her poems reveal an increasing sense of guilt, as if she blamed herself for ever taking her brother to Thorp Green.

In her diary paper of 31st July 1845, Anne wrote:

Yesterday was Emily's birthday, and the time when we should
have opened our 1841 paper, but by mistake we opened it today
instead. How many things have happened since it was written—
some pleasant, some far otherwise. Yet I was then at Thorp
Green, and now I am only just escaped from it. I was wishing to
leave it then, and if I had known that I had four years longer
to stay how wretched I should have been; but during my stay
I had some very unpleasant and undreamt of experiences of
human nature. Others have seen more changes. Charlotte has
left Mr White's and been twice to Brussels, where she stayed
each time nearly a year. Emily has been there too and stayed
nearly a year. Branwell has left Luddenden Foot, and had much
tribulation and ill-health. He was very ill on Thursday, but he
went with John Brown to Liverpool, where he is now I suppose
and we hope he will be better and do better in future. This is
a dismal, cloudy, wet evening. We have had so far a very cold,
wet summer. Charlotte has lately been to Hathersage, in Derby-
shire, on a visit of three weeks to Ellen Nussey. She is now sitting
sewing in the dining-room. Emily is ironing upstairs. I am sitting
in the dining-room in the rocking chair before the fire with my
feet on the fender. Papa is in the parlour. Tabby and Martha are,
I think, in the kitchen. Keeper and Flossy are I do not know
where. Little Dick is hopping in his cage. When the last paper
was written we were thinking of setting up a school. The scheme
has been dropt, and long after taken up again and dropt again
because we could not get pupils. Charlotte is thinking of getting
another situation. She is wishing to go to Paris. Will she go?
She has let Flossy in, by the way, and he is now lying on the
sofa. Emily is engaged in writing the Emperor Julius's Life. She
has read some of it and I want very much to hear the rest. She
is writing some poetry too. I wonder what it is about? I have
begun the third volume of *Passages in The Life of an Individual*
I wish I had finished it. This afternoon I began to set about
making my grey figured silk frock that was dyed at Keighley.
What sort of hand shall I make of it; E. and I have a great deal
of work to do. When shall we sensibly diminish it? It want to
get a habit of early rising. Shall I succeed? We have not yet
finished our Gondal Chronicles that we began three years and
a half ago. When will they be done? The Gondals are at present
in sad state. The Republicans are uppermost, but the Royalists
are not quite overcome. The young sovereigns, with their
brothers and sisters are still at the Palace of Instruction. The
Unique Society, about half a year ago, were wrecked on a desert

island as they were returning from Gaaldine. They are still there, but we have not played at them much yet. The Gondals in general are not in first-rate playing condition. Will they improve? I wonder how we shall all be, and where and how situated, on the thirtieth of July 1848, when, if we are all alive, Emily will be just 30. I shall be in my 29th year, Charlotte in her 33rd, and Branwell in his 32nd, and what changes shall we have seen and known; and shall we be much changed ourselves? I hope not, for the worst at least. I, for my part, cannot well be flatter or older in mind than I am now. Hoping for the best, I conclude.

Apart from its sentimental interest as the last diary paper that has been found, it is intrinsically valuable, because it reveals clearly Anne's state of mind.

Anne begins by referring briefly and cryptically to events at Thorp Green. She described the weather, which seems to match her own mood. She pinpoints the whereabouts of her family and of her pets. She mentions neither William Weightman, Martha Taylor, nor Aunt Branwell. Reticence probably closed her lips with regard to the first two, but Aunt Branwell, who reared Anne from babyhood, is not granted one syllable of remembrance or regret. Instead, she relates that her feet are on the fender and that the dog is lying on the sofa—two things never permitted during Aunt Branwell's reign.

It is learned that Emily is writing a prose tale and presumably reading it aloud to Anne, but she is not sharing her poetry, about which Anne is naturally curious.

Anne, herself, finds little escape in writing—she is weary of her prose tale, and has little interest in the fate of the Gondals. The infernal world cannot compensate for the miseries of the real world.

Anne, apparently, fills her days with a multitude of trivialities, but the overall impression left by the paper is an impression of complete dejection.

NOTES TO CHAPTER TWELVE

1. Anne's Birthday Note for 1841.
2. Charlotte repeated the observations in a letter to Ellen Nussey as late as 1844.

3. Mrs Gaskell repeated the allegations as if it were proven fact in her *Life of Charlotte Brontë*.
4. Her personal fortune amounted to £6,000. She subscribed regularly to four charities including the S.P.C.K. She also belonged to a local Circulating Library, paying two guineas annually.
5. Letter from Branwell Brontë to William Grundy, 1845.
6. This fact, hitherto overlooked by biographers, was commented upon by Daphne du Maurier in *The Infernal World of Branwell Brontë*.
7. Poem by Anne Brontë, dated 20th May 1845.
8. Winifred Gerin makes this point in her biography of *Anne Brontë*.
9. Birthday Paper by Anne Brontë, dated 30th July 1845.
10. Letter from Mr Robinson to Mr Brontë.
11. These facts were noted in *Scarborough Herald*, 10th July 1845.
12. The story 'Corner Dishes' has also been attributed to Branwell himself.
13. This is a well-founded tradition, mentioned by both Charlotte and Branwell.

THIRTEEN

Currer, Ellis and Acton Bell

My birthday—showery, breezy, cool. I am twenty-seven years old today. This morning Anne and I opened the papers we wrote four years since, on my twenty-third birthday. This paper, we intend, if all be well, to open on my thirtieth—three years hence, 1848. Since the 1841 paper the following events have taken place. Our school scheme has been abandoned, and instead Charlotte and I went to Brussels on the 8th February, 1842.

Branwell left his place at Luddenden Foot. C. and I returned from Brussels, November 8th, 1842, in consequence of aunt's death.

Branwell went to Thorp Green as a tutor, where Anne still continued, January, 1843.

Charlotte returned to Brussels the same month, and after staying a year, came back again on New Year's Day, 1844.

Anne left her situation at Thorp Green of her own accord, June, 1845.

Anne and I went our first long journey by ourselves together, leaving home on the 30th June, Monday, sleeping at York, returning to Keighley, Tuesday evening, sleeping there and walking home on Wednesday morning. Though the weather was broken we enjoyed ourselves very much, except during a few hours at Bradford. And during our excursion we were, Ronald Macalgin, Henry Angorra, Juliet Augusteena, Rosabella Esmalden, Ella and Juliet Egremont, Catherine Navarre, and Cordelie Fitz-aphnold, escaping from the palaces of instruction to join the Royalists who are hard driven at present by the victorious Republicans. The Gondals still flourish bright as ever. I am at present writing a work on the First Wars—Anne has been writing some articles on this, and a book by Henry Sophona—we intend sticking firm by the rascals as long as they delight us which I am glad to say they do at present. I should have mentioned that last summer the school scheme was revived in full vigour—We had prospectuses printed, dispatched letters to all acquaintances imparting our plans, and did our little all but it was found no go—now I don't desire a school at all, and none of us have any great longing for it. We have cash enough for our present wants, with a prospect of accumulation—We are all in decent health, only that papa has a complaint in his eyes and with the exception of B. who I hope will be better and do better, hereafter. I am quite contented for myself—not as idle as formerly, altogether as hearty and having learnt to make the most of the present and hope for the future with less fidgetiness that I cannot do all I wish—seldom or ever troubled with nothing to do, and merely desiring that everybody could be as comfortable as myself and as undesponding, and then we should have a very tolerable world of it.

By mistake I find we have opened the paper on the 31st instead of the 30th. Yesterday was much such a day as this, but the morning was divine—

Tabby who was gone in our last paper is come back and has lived with us two years and a half and is in good health.— Martha, who also departed, is here too—We have got Flossy, got and lost Tiger—lost the hawk, Hero, which with the geese was given away, and is doubtless dead, for when I came back from Brussels I enquired on all hands and could hear nothing of him. Tiger died early last year—Keeper and Flossy are well, also the canary acquired some four years since. We are now all at home, and likely to be there some time. Branwell went to Liverpool on Tuesday to stay a week. Tabby has just been teasing me to turn as formerly to 'pilloputate'.

Anne and I should have picked the black currants if it had been fine and sunny. I must hurry off now to my turning and ironing. I have plenty of work on hands, and writing, and am altogether full of business. With best wishes for the whole house till 1848, July 30th, and as much longer as may be. I conclude.[1]

In view of the circumstances, this diary paper is startling. From beginning to end, the tone is one of buoyancy and hope. A reader unacquainted with the events of 1845 would be excused for imagining that all was well in the Brontë world. The whole point is, all *was* well in Emily's own particular world. Charlotte, still agonizing after her professor, might scheme uselessly to travel to new scenes and faces in Paris. Anne might mourn over her lost love and her failure to help Branwell. Emily was happy, untouched by the misery of those about her. The secret of her strength was Gondal.

Emily created Gondal out of her own being, moving freely through its wild, bleak landscapes, its palaces, and attendant islands, even while she busied herself with tasks about the Parsonage. She was well aware that Gondal was not an actual world, that it existed only within her imagination, that she could end the game if she chose to do so. But imagination can conceive of a reality above and beyond physical reality. There was, even, a reality beyond Gondal itself—a reality of which she caught sudden, searing glimpses.

A woman who could write, in a little, private notebook

> Though Earth and moon were gone
> And suns and universes ceased to be
> And thou were left alone
> Every Existence would exist in thee.
>
> There is not room for Death
> Nor atom that his might could render void
> Since thou are Being and Breath
> And what thou art may never be destroyed.[2]

was not going to waste her energy in grief over a wayward brother.

This is not to suggest that Emily was indifferent to the sufferings of others, for there is a strong tradition that she, of all the sisters, afforded Branwell the most practical assistance. Suffering was a part of this world, and she accepted it, just as she accepted her household duties, the failure of the school plan and Aunt Branwell's death. She is, indeed, so occupied that her birthday can pass by without her or the family apparently noticing or caring.

Branwell returned from Liverpool in no better shape than he had gone to it. Even a trip to North Wales had failed to revive him, but it had, at least, given him time in which to assemble the facts of his story.

Not until October, four months after his dismissal, did he write to his friend, Grundy, with the first accounts of events at Thorp Green. True or false, Branwell believed in his story to the end of his life. He was now the central figure of a tragic love affair, and his sufferings were confided in the highly emotional accents of a Gothic romance.[3]

My admiration of her mental and personal attractions, my knowledge of her unselfish sincerity, her sweet temper, and unwearied care for others, with but unrequited return where most should have been given—although she is seventeen years my senior, all combined to an attachment on my part, and led to reciprocations which I had little looked for. During nearly three years I had daily "troubled pleasure" soon chastised by fear. Three months since, I received a furious letter from my employer, threatening to shoot me if I returned from my vacation, which I was passing at home; and letters from her lady's-maid and physician informed me of the outbreak, only checked by her firm courage and resolution that whatever harm came to her none should come to me.

To do him justice, Branwell was not spending all his days drinking and grieving. He was making valiant efforts to be reinstated on the railway,[4] and he had begun to write a novel. Called *The Weary Are At Rest*, it was destined never to be completed. Its author lacked the sheer self-discipline necessary to continue his tale, but the fragment that remains is interesting.

Its hero is none other than Alexander Percy, Earl of Northangerland—Branwell's other self. Percy is staying at the country house of Mr and Mrs Thurston, and falls in love with his hostess. Her Christian name is Maria, so that one is suddenly confused, as Branwell doubtless was, by an old and tragic memory.

In order to win the reluctant Maria, Percy resorts to a spectacular piece of tomfoolery, by borrowing a local chapel for a Dissenter's Meeting. At this meeting, he appeals dramatically for mission funds, hoping his religious fervour will win the lady's heart.

Apparently, he is successful, for Percy and Maria return from a walk in the shrubberies and excite suspicion by their fond glances.

And *The Weary Are At Rest* was never finished. Inspiration still came in flashes to the author, but it was too late for him to weld his ideas into a coherent whole.

Branwell's sisters had no idea that he was trying to write. According to Charlotte, "he will do nothing but drink and make us all wretched".[5] He was not only drinking but drugging himself too, seeking a refuge in the bright shadows of artificially-induced fantasy.

It is extremely doubtful if he ever knew of the discovery that Charlotte made in the autumn of 1845—a discovery that was to change the course of their lives.

One day in the autumn of 1845, I accidentally alighted on a M.S. volume of verse, in my sister Emily's handwriting. Of course, I was not surprised, knowing that she could and did write verse; I looked it over, and something more than surprise seized me—a deep conviction that these were not common effusions, nor at all like the poetry women generally write. I thought them condensed and terse, vigorous and genuine. To my ear, they had also a peculiar music—wild, melancholy and elevating.

My sister Emily was not a person of demonstrative character, nor one on the recesses of whose mind and feelings even those nearest and dearest to her could, with impunity, intrude unlicensed; it took hours to reconcile her to the discovery I made, and days to persuade her that such poems merited publication. I knew, however, that a mind like hers could not be without some latent spark of honourable ambition, and refused to be discouraged in my attempts to fan that spark to flame.

Meantime, my younger sister quietly produced some of her own compositions, intimating that, since Emily's had given me pleasure, I might like to look at hers. I could not but be a partial judge, yet I thought that these verses too, had a sweet sincere pathos of their own.[6]

One wonders how Charlotte came "accidentally" upon the poems. One also wonders if the "spark of honourable ambition" was as latent as she supposed.

Emily was incapable of showing her work openly, but it is very likely that she would choose this way of displaying her poems—by leaving them where Charlotte could find them—not perhaps with a definite view of publication, but because even she, solitary and self-sufficient as she was, must have craved some measure of outside criticism.

It may have taken days to persuade Emily that they were worth publication, but if she had wished to keep her work secret, she need never have agreed to her writings being made public. She had written for her own pleasure, but having ensured that her personal identity would remain hidden, she was quite ready to revise her poetry and to present it to the world.

Choosing to retain their own initials, they decided upon the pseudonyms: Currer, Ellis and Acton Bell. Such names had a bi-sexual quality which would prevent their being recognized immediately as 'women writers' and labelled accordingly.

It was not easy to find a publisher even willing to print the books at the author's own expense, but eventually Messrs Aylott and Jones, of Paternoster Row, London, agreed to do so for a fee of thirty guineas. The sum was made up between them, from their savings and the residue of Aunt Branwell's legacy. The venture was kept secret. This was a fairly simple matter, for Branwell slept most of the day, and Mr Brontë could not see well enough to read. With the two servants in the kitchen, and Branwell either in his room, or down at the 'Black Bull', they felt secure enough to sit round the dining-room table, carefully editing and arranging their verses.

In the first week of May 1846, the slender volume of poetry made its appearance. It was the climax of months of preparation, of dozens of letters to the publishers in which Charlotte anxiously discussed the safe arrival of the manuscripts, the choice of paper and type, and the money to be spent on advertising. Great preparations, indeed, for so paltry a return!

The book was almost ignored by Press and public alike.[7] A few reviews damning with faint praise appeared; two copies were sold, and a song writer from Warwick—a Mr Enoch— asked for the writers' autographs.

It was hardly a propitious start to a literary career, and the girls must have been bitterly disappointed. Their only cause for self-congratulation lay in the fact that nobody knew the Brontës had written the book.

Yet, discouragement could not quench the burning ambition to see their work in print. Even before the publication of the poems, Charlotte was writing to Messrs Aylott and Jones.

C. E. and A. Bell are now preparing for the press a work of fiction, consisting of three distinct and unconnected tales, which may be published either together, as a work of three volumes of the ordinary novel size, or separately as single volumes, as may be deemed most advisable.[8]

Messrs Aylott and Jones did not deal in prose tales, but they were obliging enough to send a list of publishers who did and to these firms, in turn, were sent the manuscripts of *The Professor*, *Wuthering Heights*, and *Agnes Grey*.

Those biographers, who praise the Brontës for having the courage to write novels after the failure of their poems, are giving credit where credit is not due. The tales were finished and probably even submitted, before the poems were printed. During the long winter, each sister had worked, not only upon her poetry, but upon a prose tale. According to Charlotte, they read their work aloud to one another, chapter by chapter, inviting comment and criticism.

In Emily's case this seems almost incredible. Her work may have been shown after its completion, but that she would share her moments of inspiration is very doubtful. One senses that the book she read for her sisters was a revised and expanded edition of an earlier tale, written perhaps much earlier, perhaps, at the beginning, in collaboration with Branwell.

Later, the claim was made that Branwell was, in fact, the sole author of *Wuthering Heights*.[9]

In 1867, William Dearden declared that in 1848, he, Branwell and J. B. Leyland each agreed to compose a poem or drama and read them aloud at the Cross Road's Inn, midway between Haworth and Keighley. Upon the occasion, Branwell discovered that he had, by mistake, brought the opening chapter of a novel upon which he was trying his hand. According to Dearden. Branwell proceeded to read out the first chapter of *Wuthering Heights*.

Grundy, still later, in 1879, "took up the argument declaring that Branwell had asserted that *Wuthering Heights* was his own production".

The very fact that Dearden waited until the Brontës and Leyland were dead, before bringing out this statement, casts immediate doubt upon its validity. Even if the incident did take place, two possibilities still remain. Either Branwell had brought his sister's manuscript by mistake, or he actually did read a draft upon which he and Emily had collaborated.

If so, it would have been merely a draft, for at no time was Branwell capable of writing the ice-cold prose, the closely-knit texture, of the novel acclaimed by all critics as a masterpiece of literature. But he could easily have dreamed up the original idea of the arch-fiends, bound to each other by a chain stronger than death.

Grundy may, indeed, have been informed that Branwell was the author of the novel. Charlotte believed, all her life, that her brother never knew they had published a line. If Branwell did know, then it is quite likely that, rather than admit to his friends he had been excluded from the secret, he would attempt to pass off the novel as his own among his cronies.

If Branwell knew that his sisters were attempting to publish their works, it is very doubtful if he paid much attention. Soon his own affairs were engrossing him far more than any work of fiction could do.

NOTES TO CHAPTER THIRTEEN

1. Birthday Paper of 1845 by Emily Brontë.
2. Poem by Emily Brontë, 2nd January 1846.
3. Letter from Branwell Brontë to William Grundy, October 1845.
4. Letter from Branwell Brontë to Secretary of the Manchester and Hebden Bridge Railway Company, 23rd October 1845.
5. Letter from Charlotte Brontë to Ellen Nussey.
6. Charlotte Brontë, Biographical Notice of Ellis and Acton Bell.
7. Reviews appeared in *Atheneum* and *Dublin University Magazine*.
8. Letter from Charlotte Brontë to Messrs Aylott and Jones, 6th April 1846.
9. Letter from William Dearden to *Halifax Guardian*, 15th June 1867.

FOURTEEN

A Trip to Manchester

On 26th May, the Rev. Edmund Robinson died at Thorp Green of "Dyspepsia many years Phthisis 3 months". According to local tradition, when Branwell heard of Mr Robinson's death, he danced through the graveyard like a mad thing. But the death may not have been the cause for rejoicing that it was thought to be.

For almost a year, Branwell had represented himself as a lover, parted from his mistress only by a jealous husband. It was a situation in the romantic Angrian tradition. Branwell believed in it implicitly. How far his family did so is a matter for conjecture.

When Mr Robinson died it was naturally expected that, after a decent interval, Branwell would marry his Lydia. He had, after all, presented her as sick for love of him, held in bondage by a jealous mate.

Unfortunately, Lydia Robinson suddenly became available. She was no longer the imprisoned heroine, but a wealthy, attractive widow. There was nothing to prevent Branwell from claiming his love, except Mrs Robinson and Branwell himself.

The version of the story which was, for years, considered to be the truth was put about by Branwell. He declared that the terms of Mr Robinson's will would prevent their marriage, as her late husband had decreed that if she resumed her liaison with Branwell Brontë she would lose both her inheritance and the custody of her children.

There was, of course, no truth in the tale.

No mention was made of the children, and, in the event of her remarriage, Lydia Robinson would merely forfeit the actual inheritance derived from her husband. Of her private fortune, she retained full control.

The question remains whether Branwell knew the truth or not. Within a few days, he was summoned to the 'Black Bull', where Gooch, Mrs Robinson's coachman, waited with a verbal message. What passed between them is not known. Some time later the barmaid heard a noise "like the bleating of a calf", and going into the room found Branwell on the floor in a fit.

It was generally assumed that the news about the will had brought on an attack of epilepsy. If Mrs Robinson had wished to keep Branwell at arm's length, she could not have achieved a better way of doing so.

It is, however, by no means certain, that Branwell had ever loved Mrs Robinson. In that event, she would scarcely have bothered to invent the story of the will. One wonders what message Gooch brought. If it was not to inform Branwell of the will, what other news could throw him into an epileptic fit? Was it something concerning Edmund, now tucked away with a new, moral tutor?

Branwell told his family and friends, in letters weeping with self-pity, that his hopes of marrying the widow were shattered, not merely by the terms of the will, but by her own agonized state of mind.

On 17th June, Charlotte wrote to Ellen Nussey:

> To Papa he allows rest neither day nor night, and he is con-
> tinually screwing money out of him, sometimes threatening that
> he will kill himself if it is withheld from him. He says Mrs Robin-
> son is now insane, that her mind is a complete wreck owing to
> remorse for her conduct towards Mr Robinson (whose end it
> appears was hastened by distress of mind) and grief for having
> lost him. I do not know how much to believe of what he says,
> but I fear she is very ill.[1]

Ellen Nussey would understand something of what the Brontës were enduring, for one of Ellen's brothers recently had been committed to an asylum, after having been nursed at home. Ellen would understand, too, the havoc wrought in a quiet household by a violent drunkard.

Branwell luxuriated in his misery, painting lurid pictures of the heart-rending state of his beloved.

> She, too, surrounded by powerful persons who hate me like Hell, has sunk into religious melancholy, believes that her weight of sorrow is God's punishment, and hopelessly resigns herself to her doom.[2]

A truly pathetic situation! Unhappily, Mrs Robinson was at that time enjoying the sea air at Whitby, and none of the letters describing her alleged suffering have survived, although Branwell maintained that he was in correspondence with her doctors. He was, indeed, writing to her doctors, not to enquire the state of Mrs Robinson's health, but to obtain money with which to pay his debts.[3]

If Branwell truly loved Mrs Robinson, as he affirmed, he would scarcely have been induced to remain away from her by bribery, particularly if he already believed in her insanity. Yet Branwell was receiving considerable sums of money from the hands of her physician, Dr Crosby. The money could not have been paid with the object of keeping Branwell silent, for the Thorp Green scandal was ringing around Haworth. Had Branwell threatened to reveal something else—something besides which adultery would appear a minor crime?

All one can be certain about, in attempting to analyse Branwell's state of mind, is his despair.

> I know only that it is time for me to be something when I am nothing. That my father cannot have long to live, and that when he dies, my evening which is already twilight, will become night —That I shall then have a constitution so strong it will keep me years in torture and despair when I should every hour pray that I might die.[4]

There could be no question of any of the sisters leaving home. Mr Brontë had moved into Branwell's bedroom, to try to control him during the night. Charlotte wrote despairing letters to Ellen Nussey, in which the brother she had once idolized was condemned as a drunken wastrel, a man upon whom sympathy would have been utterly useless.

(*above*) The sitting-room at the parsonage, showing the couch where
Emily Brontë died. (*below*) Higher Withens, near Haworth (the site
of *Wuthering Heights*)

Elizabeth Cleghorn
Gaskell, by George
Richmond

The Duke of Wellington

Anne grieved over the alteration in the family circumstances, writing sad little verses about the misery they now endured.

> The fire is burning in the grate
> As redly as it used to burn;
> But still the hearth is desolate
> Till mirth, and love, with *peace* return.[5]

The tradition has arisen that of the three sisters, Emily was the only one to stand by Branwell in his extremity. Charlotte certainly washed her hands of him, and Anne's delicate health would effectually prevent her from being of much practical use. Emily was the tallest in the family, and the least emotional. She would, naturally, be the one who waited up for her brother's stumbling return from the 'Black Bull'. It was Emily alone who had the physical strength to drag Branwell upstairs. The only recorded comment she ever made was to inform Charlotte that he was "a hopeless being".[6] There is an air of resigned acceptance in the phrase.

Emily's physical strength was called upon more than once. One afternoon, when Emily and Anne were in the Parsonage, Anne went upstairs to where Branwell lay in a drugged stupor, to discover that her brother had overturned a candle and had set the bedclothes on fire. Anne tried, unavailingly, to drag him from the bed, but he was too heavy and she was forced to shriek for Emily. Emily came at once, picked Branwell up bodily and threw him into a corner of the room, then quenched the flames with pitchers of water from the washstand. Only then did she turn to Anne and say, calmly: "We had better not worry Papa with this."

To this period, also, belonged her famous tussle with Keeper and her adventure with the mad dog.

Keeper, a gigantic bull-mastiff, had been given to Emily by a local farmer, with the warning that the animal was faithful and obedient unless struck by a stick. Keeper proved true to his nature. He sat by Emily at table waiting for a share of her breakfast, walked with her over the moors, and even condescended to perform tricks for his mistress. His one fault was a habit of lying on the bed where his paws soiled the carefully laundered counterpane. Emily finally declared that if the incident occurred again, she would deal with the dog severely.

H

The very next day, Tabby came in, trembling but trium-
phant, to inform Emily that Keeper was once again lying on
the bed. Emily went upstairs and reappeared, dragging the
growling beast by the collar. She planted him at the foot of
the stairs, while Anne and Charlotte watched silently, afraid
to distract her attention. There was no time for her to fetch
a stick, because, the moment she loosed her grip Keeper sprang
at her throat. Her clenched fist met him in mid-leap, and she
then proceeded to beat the animal into unconsciousness with
her bare hands.

It was an act of animal savagery, which has horrified Brontë
admirers, but it did show Emily's implacable nature and her
strength.

Another event served to illustrate her self-possession in the
face of crisis. Going to the backyard to give a drink of water
to a passing dog, she was bitten by the animal. A few moments
later, some passing farm labourers called to her that she should
chain up Keeper as there was a mad dog at large. Returning to
the kitchen, where the Italian irons were heating ready for
ironing, she applied the white-hot tip to the bite, cauterizing
the wound herself. When Tabby met Charlotte and Anne, who
were returning from the village, with an excited account of
the incident, Emily was calmly ironing, with a handkerchief
round her arm, and merely told them not to make a fuss.[7]

Such a woman would be eminently suitable for the nursing
of a sick and mentally disturbed patient, particularly if that
patient was her own brother, and even more particularly, if
that brother was sexually abnormal in the same way that Emily
was, or believed herself to be.

The sisters therefore remained at home, in an isolation now
self-imposed, for they dare not ask even Ellen Nussey to stay
lest Branwell's behaviour should spoil her visit.

The poems had failed, not only artistically but financially,
too. Aunt Branwell's legacy was running low. Part of it had
been invested, at Emily's desire, in railway shares. Most of it
was being spent to pay Branwell's debts.

Nothing happens at Haworth—nothing at least of a pleasant
kind—one little incident indeed occurred about a week ago to
sting us to life—It was merely the arrival of a Sheriff's Officer
on a visit to Branwell—inviting him either to pay his debts or

to take a trip to York. Of course his debts had to be paid—it is not agreeable to lose money time after time in this way, but it is ten times worse to witness the shabbiness of his behaviour on such occasions.[8]

The three prose tales were still being returned from publisher after publisher, and sent out again, still in the same brown paper wrappings, with the previous destination economically and naïvely crossed out.

Mr Brontë's sight was now so feeble that an operation was advised. He was still led up into the pulpit to preach, but much of the parish work was undertaken by his curate, Arthur Bell Nicholls. This serious, sallow-faced Irishman was considered to be very worthy, but Charlotte thought him humourless and severe. Her personal dislike of the man was in no way diminished by a rumour that she was about to become engaged to him.

On this matter, she wrote sharply, to Ellen:

Who gravely asked you whether Miss Brontë was not going to be married to her father's curate? I scarcely need to say that never was rumour more unfounded. It puzzles me to think how it could possibly have originated. A cold far-away sort of civility are the only terms on which I have even been with Mr Nicholls. I could by no means think of mentioning such a rumour to him even as a joke. It would make me the laughing-stock of himself and his fellow curates for half a year to come. They regard me as an old maid, and I regard them, one and all, as highly uninteresting specimens of the coarser sex.[9]

The gay flirtations of the William Weightman days were over. Ellen had made a mistake in even trying to revive them. Charlotte had accepted the fact that she would never marry. Her letters to Monsieur Heger had finally ceased. Madame Heger had objected so violently to the continued correspondence, that Heger suggested Charlotte should send her letters to an accommodation address.[10] The suggestion, with its attendant implications of furtiveness and secrecy, shocked her into silence. The letters ceased. It is impossible to guess how long it was before Charlotte's love finally starved to death for lack of nourishment.

In August 1846, Charlotte accompanied her father to Manchester to consult an eye specialist. Emily and Anne were left to deal with Branwell—a necessity which caused Charlotte great anxiety. She was also worried by the problem of house-keeping, for no meals were provided in the lodgings.

> For ourselves I could contrive—papa's diet is so very simple; but there will be a nurse coming in a day or two, and I am afraid of not having things good enough for her. Papa requires nothing you know but plain beef and mutton, tea and bread and butter; but a nurse will probably expect to live much better.[11]

The eye-specialist, Mr Wilson, performed the operation immediately.

Charlotte wrote to Ellen:

> The affair lasted precisely a quarter of an hour; it was not the simple operation of couching, but the more complicated one of extracting the cataract. Papa displayed extraordinary patience and firmness; the surgeons seemed surprised. I was in the room all the time as it was his wish that I should be there; of course I neither spoke nor moved till the thing was done, and then I felt that the less I said, either to Papa or the surgeons, the better.[12]

Mr Brontë and Charlotte remained in Manchester for a month. During that time, Mr Brontë spent most of the day in a darkened room. Charlotte had ample leisure in which to write.

A theme had been evolving in her mind—not a sober, restrained tale such as she had deliberately limited herself to in *The Professor*, but a story in which she could give rein to some of her highest flights of imagination.

In the sitting-room of her modest lodgings, Charlotte took her pen in hand and wrote:

> There was no possibility of taking a walk that day. We had been wandering, indeed, in the leafless shrubbery an hour in the morning; but since dinner (Mrs Reed, when there was no company, dined early) the cold winter wind had brought with it clouds so sombre, and a rain so penetrating, that further outdoor exercise was now out of the question.[13]

In such an unpropitious setting *Jane Eyre* was born, but she had been conceived long before, in the mind of an eight-year-old child who watched, silently, as her elder sister stood in the midst of her school-fellows, with an insulting placard tied to her pinafore.

NOTES TO CHAPTER FOURTEEN

1. Letter from Charlotte Brontë to Ellen Nussey.
2. Letter from Branwell Brontë to William Grundy.
3. Letter from Branwell Brontë to J. B. Leyland, July 1848.
4. Letter from Branwell Brontë to J. B. Leyland, 24th January 1847.
5. 'Domestic Peace', poem by Anne Brontë, dated Monday night, 11th May 1846.
6. See letter from Charlotte Brontë to Ellen Nussey.
7. These three incidents were related by Charlotte Brontë to Mrs Gaskell.
8. Letter from Charlotte Brontë to Ellen Nussey, 13th December 1846.
9. Letter from Charlotte Brontë to Ellen Nussey
10. Monsieur Heger rather surprisingly told this fact to Mrs Gaskell.
11. Letter from Charlotte Brontë to Ellen Nussey
12. Letter from Charlotte Brontë to Ellen Nussey
13. Charlotte Brontë, *Jane Eyre*, Chapter 1.

FIFTEEN

Jane Eyre

Charlotte returned to Haworth, with a thick bundle of manuscript, to which she added further chapters at a steady rate throughout the long, cold winter of 1846. She, of all three sisters, had the least to hope for. *The Professor* was still being rejected by publishers. Emily and Anne had been more fortunate. Both *Agnes Grey* and *Wuthering Heights* were accepted for publication by Thomas Newby of Mortimer Street, London, on condition that the authors paid part of the cost of printing.

Emily and Anne had accepted the terms and forwarded the required sum of fifty pounds. The exact date of acceptance is unknown, but was probably in the late winter of 1846 or the early months of 1847. A puzzle immediately presents itself.

Charlotte informed Mrs Gaskell that it was their custom to discharge their household duties before the evening, and then to sit around the dining-room table and write. Anne was already working on her second novel, *The Tenant of Wildfell Hall.* Emily was also writing, but all traces of the work on which she was engaged have vanished. They may have been destroyed. They may still be lying in the bottom of some dusty drawer. Stranger things have happened.

Ellen Nussey, close friend though she was, knew nothing of the fever of creation that possessed Charlotte and her sisters. Ellen had never set foot in the infernal world, never glimpsed the erotic delights of Angria or the savage splendours of Gondal. Charlotte's letters contained only news of events at the Parsonage connected with Branwell or Mr Brontë. Health was also uppermost in her mind. All of them had suffered from continual colds, but Anne's vitality was noticeably impaired.

> Poor Anne has suffered greatly from asthma, but is now, we are glad to say, rather better. She had two nights last week when her cough and difficulty of breathing were painful indeed to hear and witness and must have been more distressing to suffer; she bore it, as she bears all afflictions, without one complaint, only sighing now and then when nearly worn out. She has extraordinary heroism and endurance. I admire, but I certainly could not imitate her.[1]

Anne herself received some pleasure when letters from Mrs Robinson's daughters suddenly arrived. She had lost touch with her former pupils and this unexpected resumption of friendship pleased her.

The Robinson girls were able to give their ex-governess an exact account of their mother's activities. Their elder sister had eloped some time previously with an actor, called Henry Roxby, and had been cut off with a shilling for her pains. The younger girls were also engaged to be married, but neither professed the slightest affection for her fiancé.[2]

Mrs Robinson was contemplating matrimony herself again. She was being wooed by the recently widowed Sir Edward Scott, and as her daughters disapproved of the match, she naturally wished to get them off her hands as speedily as possible.

Charlotte told Ellen that they took care to keep the Anne-Robinson correspondence a secret from Branwell. Her brother was still declaring that Mrs Robinson was insane for love of him. He had adopted the pose of tragic lover and to stick to it became a necessity, but it is doubtful if he was completely unaware of her activities.

Mrs Robinson was, after all, a society woman whose doings were regularly reported in the newspapers and Branwell was not always confined to his room. When he had money in his pocket he could visit Leyland or Grundy who doubtless informed him of the current gossip, but to admit that he believed it would have meant admitting reality into the shadowy world where he dwelt.

Charlotte, who had forbidden Ellen Nussey to visit Haworth, now decided to risk an invitation. She longed to see her friend, who had not been near the Parsonage since Branwell's dismissal from Thorp Green, and she thought there was a possibility of the visit being free from embarrassment.

> Branwell is quieter now and for a good reason; he has got to the end of a considerable sum of money—You must expect to find him weaker in mind, and the complete rake in appearance. I have no apprehensions of his being at all uncivil to you; on the contrary, he will be as smooth as oil.[3]

Unfortunately, Ellen's visit was cancelled, not because Branwell became violent again, but because family responsibilities kept Charlotte's friend at home.

The following month, surplus copies of the volume of poems published the previous year, were dispatched to Wordsworth, Tennyson, Lockhart and De Quincey. With each copy went the following letter, meant to be humorous but revealing bitter disappointment.

> Sir,
> My relatives Ellis and Acton Bell, and myself, heedless of the repeated warnings of various respectable publishers, have committed the rash act of printing a volume of poems.
> The consequences predicted have, of course, overtaken us; our book is found to be a drug; no man needs it or heeds it. In the space of a year our publisher has disposed but of two copies, and by what painful efforts he succeeded in getting rid of these two, himself only knows.
> Before transferring the edition to the trunkmakers, we have decided on distributing as presents a few copies of what we cannot sell; and we beg to offer you one in acknowledgement of the pleasure and profit we have often derived from your works.
>
> > I am, Sir,
> > Yours very respectfully,
> > Currer Bell.

If the gifts were ever acknowledged by the recipients, none of the letters has survived.

In August 1847, *The Professor* arrived back at the Parsonage again, rejected once more but in such kindly terms that "it cheered the author better than a vulgarly expressed acceptance would have done".[4]

Messrs Smith and Elder, the publishers in question, considered *The Professor* to be too quiet for current taste, but were interested in any other manuscript that the writer might care to offer.

Charlotte immediately parcelled up the recently completed *Jane Eyre* and sent it to them. The book was read first by W. S. Williams, the firm's Reader, who waxed so enthusiastic over it that the head of the publishing house, George Smith, took it home with him over the weekend.

George Smith began to glance through the manuscript after breakfast on Sunday morning and was soon immersed in it to such an extent that he hastily cancelled a prior luncheon engagement and ordered sandwiches instead of a cooked dinner.

The novel was accepted immediately, for an outright sale of five hundred pounds—a sum that made Charlotte "glad and proud". She was paying a long delayed visit to Ellen Nussey at Brookroyd when the proofs arrived for correction. Nothing was said on the subject. Charlotte corrected her proof-sheets while Ellen did some sewing, and the delicate tact of the one never intruded upon the reticence of the other.

On 16th October, *Jane Eyre* by Currer Bell was published. It was an immediate success, and has remained a success ever since.

The story itself is one of tremendous and sustained interest and excitement. Anybody who follows the events of the first few chapters is compelled to complete their reading, if only to discover the eventual fate of the orphan, Jane. Charlotte's delineation of the character was perfect. One dreads to imagine the sentimentality with which Dickens would have drawn the portrait of the unloved child, but Jane Eyre is no Oliver Twist or Little Nell. She is a quick-witted, rebellious little girl, who believes in standing up for her rights and is perfectly capable of impertinence. One senses, from the beginning, that the heroine will eventually fall on her feet.

Seldom can personal experience and popular idiom have been so successfully fused together. Into her tale, Charlotte had incorporated her painful childhood memories of Cowan Bridge, her love for an older man, her personal and secret convictions that a plain, poor and friendless girl has the right, not only to fall in love, but to declare her love in terms that a well-bred Victorian maiden would have blushed to use.

> "Do you think I can stay to become nothing to you? Do you think I am an automaton?—a machine without feelings? You think wrong!—I have as much soul as you—and full as much heart! And if God had gifted me with some beauty and much wealth, I should have made it as hard for you to leave me, as it is now for me to leave you. I am not talking to you now through the medium of custom, conventionalities, nor even of mortal flesh, it is my spirit that addresses your spirit, just as if both had passed through the grave, and we stood at God's feet, equal as we are!"[5]

In just such words must Charlotte have longed to address Monsieur Heger.

The Gothic elements of *Jane Eyre* were calculated to appeal to the popular taste. Secret passages, chained lunatics, mysterious fires and supernatural voices were then desirable ingredients for a best-selling novel. That they also formed part of Charlotte's infernal world merely served to integrate them more securely into the fabric of her tale. They never became sensational appendages, but are accepted by the readers as a natural development to the plot.

Only when the last page is turned, does reality intrude, to question the incredible coincidences, to ask how on earth a sensible man manages to engage such a careless keeper for his lunatic wife. But Charlotte's world had its own reality. Those who read *Jane Eyre* accept it, despite the melodrama and improbabilities, as truth.

Not everybody thought the novel to be a masterpiece. George Searle Phillips, writing in the *Leeds Times*, declared:

> The foundation of the story is bad, the characters ill-drawn and the feelings false and unnatural. If our readers be induced by our remark to peruse the novel before us they are welcome to undertake the task, and much good it may do them.

There were hundreds to accept the invitation—to immerse themselves in the life story of a provincial governess. The fact

that parts of the novel were considered indelicate, merely served
to whet the public's appetite.

The name 'Currer Bell' was, of course, completely unknown
in literary circles. It was correctly guessed to be a pseudonym,
and the identity of Mr Bell became a talking point up and down
the country. It was even assumed that the book had been
written by an established writer, and both Thackeray and
Dickens were forced to issue denials that they had had any
hand in its production.

At the Parsonage, life moved along at its usual, monotonous
pace, enlivened only by a drunken outbreak from Branwell,
who, according to Charlotte, "has been more than ordinarily
troublesome and annoying of late; he leads Papa a wretched
life".[6]

In Haworth, Currer Bell remained unknown. Some months
previously, Charlotte had been thrown into a panic when her
father met the postman in the lane, and upon being asked if a
'Currer Bell' were staying at the Parsonage, replied there was
no such person in the parish. Charlotte had immediately in-
structed her publishers to forward mail care of Miss C. Brontë,
but if the similarity of initials was ever noticed, he had the
tact to keep silent.

The girls decided to tell their father of the success of *Jane
Eyre* and the following conversation took place between Charlotte and Mr Brontë.

"Papa, I've been writing a book."

"Have you, my dear?"

"Yes, and I want you to read it."

"I am afraid it will try my eyes too much."

"But it is not in manuscript, it is printed."

"My dear! You've never thought of the expense it will be!
It will almost sure to be a loss, for how can you get a book sold?
No one knows you or your name."

"But, Papa, I don't think it will be a loss; no more will you
if you will just let me read you a review or two, and tell you
more about it."

Charlotte read about half a dozen reviews to her father,
taking care to include one or two unfavourable reports. Then
she left him with a copy of *Jane Eyre*.

Mr Brontë emerged at teatime, and called out to Emily and

Anne, "Girls, do you know Charlotte has been writing a book and it is much better than likely?"[7] Mr Brontë had had his suspicions that something was going on, but had said nothing.

Mr Brontë, reserved though he was, would probably have enjoyed relating Charlotte's success, for that success might compensate, in some measure, for Branwell's failure. But the proud old man was to be denied even a tiny boast. For Branwell's sake, the identity of Currer Bell must be kept a close secret. If Branwell knew that his sister had written a best-selling novel, the consciousness of his own disgrace might overwhelm him.

Ironically, Branwell, despite Charlotte's assertions, probably guessed something of what was happening. *Jane Eyre* was being eagerly read, even in Keighley, and if he had ever glanced at a copy, the style and contents must have been perfectly familiar to him. In the character Helen Burns he would have seen the dead Maria whose image still haunted him, while Mr Rochester was merely the Duke of Zamorna, transposed from Angria to an English country house, and mellowed by time.

If Branwell ever read *Jane Eyre* his family never knew it. He, the creator of Angria, was no longer in the confidence of his sisters. A conspiracy of silence excluded him from participation in family affairs. Conversation would end abruptly when he entered the room. Any small gesture of penance would be met with cynical indifference.

Branwell related that when he informed Charlotte, he had been in the village to see a little girl, who was dying, she gave him so cynical and incredulous a look that it wounded him like a blow in the mouth. He immediately set off for the 'Black Bull', and "made a night of it in sheer disgust and desperation. Why could they not give me some credit when I was trying to be good?"[8]

It was too late for that. Branwell's credit had already run out with Charlotte. The brother she had loved was to all intents and purposes a different being.

By the New Year of 1848, she was writing to Ellen Nussey:

Branwell has contrived by some means to get more money from the old quarter—and has led us a sad life with absurd and often intolerable conduct—Papa is harassed day and night—we have little peace—he is always sick, has two or three times fallen down in fits.[9]

Nobody seems to have breathed the word 'epilepsy'. Branwell's insomnia, lack of appetite, constant cough and spasms of threshing unconsciousness were declared to be the result of his own excesses. His sisters wrote in secret, corresponded with their publishers in secret; and, through mistaken kindness, made him more solitary than ever.

NOTES TO CHAPTER FIFTEEN

1. Letter from Charlotte Brontë to Ellen Nussey.
2. Letters from Charlotte Brontë to Ellen Nussey.
3. Letter from Charlotte Brontë to Ellen Nussey.
4. Charlotte Brontë, Biographical Notice.
5. Charlotte Brontë, Jane Eyre, Chapter 23.
6. Letter from Charlotte Brontë to Ellen Nussey.
7. Charlotte repeated this conversation verbatim to Mrs Gaskell.
8. Branwell is said to have related this to George Searle Phillips—the same Phillips who reviewed Jane Eyre so scathingly.
9. Letter from Charlotte Brontë to Ellen Nussey, 11th January 1848.

SIXTEEN

Wuthering Heights

The success of *Jane Eyre* led to the speedy publication of *Wuthering Heights* and *Agnes Grey*. They were printed in December 1847 and issued as a three-volume novel containing the two stories.

The long delay in publication had irritated Emily and Anne until Charlotte wrote on their behalf to her own publisher to ask for advice. Messrs Smith and Elder apparently offered to question Mr Newby on the subject, but their assistance was not after all required.

On 14th December Charlotte wrote to W. S. Williams, with whom she was in frequent correspondence.

"Wuthering Heights" is, I suppose, at length published, at least Mr Newby has sent the authors their six copies. I wonder how it will be received. I should say it merits the epithet "vigorous" and "original" much more than "Jane Eyre" did. "Agnes Grey" should please such critics as Mr Lewes, for it is "true" and "un-exaggerated" enough. The books are not well got up. On a former occasion I expressed my self with perhaps too little reserve regarding Mr Newby, yet I cannot but feel, and feel painfully, that Ellis and Acton have not had the justice at his hands that I have had at the hands of Messrs Smith and Elder.[1]

Emily and Anne had certainly received less than justice. Mr Newby, having hastily published the two novels, spread it about that they were earlier works by the writer of *Jane Eyre*.

The coincidence of surnames was thought to be far-fetched, and those who bought copies of the books did so mainly out of curiosity.

Neither was considered to be as good as *Jane Eyre*. Anne's tale was dismissed as a pleasant, unassuming story. The heroine, a governess like *Jane Eyre*, was written off as colourless. Her adventures were tame in comparison with the vicissitudes of fortune which befell Charlotte's creation. The book was an extended version of *Passages In The Life Of An Individual*, on which Anne had been working in 1845. Almost entirely auto-biographical in content, the novel received little attention. It was considered to be "a tale well worth telling", but not until 1936 did George Moore claim that it was "the most perfect prose narrative in English letters".[2]

To come freshly to the book today is a rewarding experience. Written in a minor key, the story abounds in delightful touches of humour, joyous descriptions of natural scenery, and wry comments upon human nature.

Inevitably, the book was compared with *Wuthering Heights*, and, just as inevitably, found wanting. This is not to say that *Wuthering Heights* was either a popular or critical success. The story revolted many people, and only one or two critics had the perspicacity to place it above *Jane Eyre*. Most of them considered the theme to be shocking, crude and sensational. Even Charlotte, the first to recognize Emily's genius, felt obliged to explain it away.

My sister's disposition, was not naturally gregarious; circumstances favoured and fostered her tendency to seclusion; except to go to church or take a walk on the hills, she rarely crossed the threshold of home. Though her feelings for the people round her was benevolent, intercourse with them she never sought; nor, with very few exceptions, ever experienced. And yet she knew them; knew their ways, their language, their family histories; she could hear of them with interest, and talk of them with detail, minute, graphic, and accurate; but *with* them she rarely exchanged a word. Hence it ensued that what her mind had gathered of the real concerning them, was too exclusively confined to those tragic and terrible traits which, in listening to the secret annals of every rude vicinage, the memory is sometimes compelled to receive the impress. Her imagination, which

was a spirit more sombre than sunny, more powerful than
sportive, found in such traits material whence it wrought
creations like Heathcliff, like Earnshaw, like Catherine. Having
formed these beings she did not know what she had done.[3]

It would be more correct to say that Charlotte did not know
what Emily had done. She was horrified by the elemental evil
which pervades even the most poetical passages, and, curiously,
missed the main point of the tale—the eventual triumph of
love over hate.

The carefully planned revenge of the fiendish gipsy is finally
prevented, not merely because his chosen victims fall in love,
but because Heathcliff himself has lost interest in his own
hatred.

Wuthering Heights inspired no school. Nobody has ever
attempted to write a sequel. It stands alone in literature; complete and perfect, inspired to some extent by local legend and
Byronic tradition; but in the main, it is a product of an imagination which does not need experience to shape it. It is a tale
which gives one an overwhelming impression of passion, yet
physical contact between Heathcliff and Catherine is actually
rare. It is a tale which appals with its sadism, yet it ends on a
note of reflective tenderness.

Charlotte complained that certain portions disturbed her
sleep, and was accused of affectation by Emily. Emily would
assuredly lose no sleep over the scenes she had written. Such
violence was a part of the Gondal world where she roamed
freely, just as she strode across the moors at home. Her characters sprang from Gondal itself, and just as Catherine Earnshaw
discovered that she *was* Heathcliff, so could Emily have cried
out that she *was* Gondal. Her lovers were not twin souls, but
possessed a single soul, so that to separate them was spiritually
impossible. It was an agony of separation which Emily had
endured during her mystical experiences and written about in
some of her poetry.

The Victorians understood none of this. They dismissed
Wuthering Heights as an early work by the author of *Jane Eyre*,
and ignored or hissed it. Emily Brontë's poems and her novel
were failures. According to Charlotte, she met the situation
with cynical indifference. If Emily had craved public acclaim,
she would never admit it. She had attempted to share the fruits

The Rev. Arthur Bell Nicholls

The Brontë Sisters, group by Jocelyn Horner

of her genius with the world, but the world rejected them. It merely confirmed her intensely pessimistic view of human nature. Henceforth, she would trust nobody, rely on nobody. She referred to her work as "rubbish" and to her poems as "those rhymes", and if she was hurt by the public indifference nobody was allowed to guess the fact.

Charlotte was busily exchanging complimentary letters with W. S. Williams, the Reader from the publishing firm.

I cannot thank you sufficiently for your letters and I can give you but a faint idea of the pleasure they afford me; they seem to introduce such light and life to the torpid retirement where we live like dormice.[4]

Charlotte was exchanging letters also with G. H. Lewes and Thackeray. For the first time in her life, she was in contact with famous men of letters. She wrote to them, of course, under the pseudonym of 'Currer Bell' and, protected by the anonymity, revealed her opinions in a frank and forthright manner.

Lewes had advised her to discipline her imagination, and to take Jane Austen as her model.

Charlotte replied, respectfully but firmly :

Why do you like Miss Austen so very much?—I had not seen "Pride and Prejudice" till I read that sentence of yours, and then I got the book. And what did I find? An accurate daguerreotyped portrait of a commonplace face; a carefully-fenced, highly-cultivated garden, with neat borders and delicate flowers; but no glance of a bright vivid physiognomy, no open country, no fresh air, no blue hill, no bonny beck. I should hardly like to live with her ladies and gentlemen, in their elegant but confined houses.[5]

Charlotte's own warmly passionate nature had nothing in common with the elegance and rapier-like wit of Jane Austen. In one respect only was their genius akin, and their affinity was one of weakness. Neither could adequately describe the joys of married life. Charlotte's imagination could not carry her beyond the altar steps. Her blunt statement, "Reader, I married him,"[6] which jars so painfully, was the statement of inexperience. Charlotte could argue, clearly and convincingly, on almost any subject. She could write of love with passionate conviction but she could not write of love's consummation. Her puritanical conscience barred her from writing of sexual matters, even if Victorian morality had not imposed its own censorship.

Early in 1848, a second edition of *Jane Eyre* was published, with a dedication to Thackeray. Charlotte wished only to honour the novelist, and neither she nor her publishers were aware that Thackeray's wife was insane. Unfortunately Thackeray was immediately identified with Mr Rochester and it was even suggested that one of the children's governesses had written *Jane Eyre* from personal experience.

Charlotte was horrified at the implication and deeply ashamed of the embarrassment she had unwittingly caused. Even the knowledge that Thackeray absolved her from any blame did not mitigate her suffering.

Miserably, Charlotte wrote to W. S. Williams:

> The very fact of his not complaining at all, and addressing me with such kindness, notwithstanding the pain and annoyance I must have caused him, increases my chagrin. I could not half express my regret to him in my answer, for I was restrained by the consciousness that that regret was just worth nothing at all— quite valueless for healing the mischief I had done.[7]

All three sisters were working now on their second novels. Charlotte had begun to write *Shirley* and Anne was writing *The Tenant of Wildfell Hall*, a task which Charlotte believed to have shortened her sister's life.

Nobody had any notion of what Emily was writing. That she was writing is strongly suggested by a letter found in her desk after her death. Near the letter was found a matching envelope addressed to "Ellis Bell, Esq.", so the natural assumption is that the letter was originally in the envelope, and therefore refers to Emily.*

Dear Sir,

I am much obliged by your kind note and shall have great pleasure in making arrangements for your next novel. I would not hurry its completion for I think you are quite right not to

---

* It has been suggested that the letter was in fact written to Acton Bell, but as it was found in Emily's desk and as the envelope was addressed to Ellis Bell, Esq., the obvious explanation is surely that both belonged together.

let it go before the world until well satisfied with it, for much depends on your next work. If it be an improvement on your first work you will have established yourself as a first-rate novelist, but if it falls short the critics will be too apt to say that you have expended your talent in your first novel. I shall therefore have pleasure in accepting it upon the understanding that its completion be at your own time.

Believe me, my dear Sir,
Yours sincerely,
T. C. Newby.
February 15th 1848.

Mr Brontë was, of course, the only one even partly in his daughters' confidence, for to outward appearances, life at the Parsonage continued its dismal, sometimes despairing, course. Branwell was still causing the family grave embarrassment, and apparently not confining his activities to the 'Black Bull'.

To Leyland, Branwell wrote:

I was *really* far enough from well when I saw you last week at Halifax, and if you should shortly happen to see Mrs Sugden of the Talbot you would greatly oblige me by telling her that I consider her conduct towards me as most kind and motherly, and that if I did anything during temporary illness to offend her I deeply regret it, and beg her to take my regret as an apology till I see her again which, I trust, will be e'er long.

I was not intoxicated when I saw you last, dear Sir, but I was so much broken down and embittered in heart that it did not need much stimulus to make me experience the fainting fit I had, after you left, at the Talbot, and another, more severe, at Mr Crowthers.[8]

The "fainting fits" are believed to have been attacks of epilepsy, but if they were recognized as such it was not admitted. Neither is it known if Branwell was, at this time, receiving medical treatment or if his father still relied on home-brewed doses, culled from the pages of his Medical Journal. Probably the family had grown so accustomed to Branwell's altered appearance that they no longer saw him clearly at all. What cannot be changed must be endured or ignored.

The three sisters were far more concerned with their own health which was, as usual, delicate. They blamed the severe frosts and east winds, but sanitary arrangements at the Parsonage were scarcely adequate.

Mr Brontë had the well cleaned by two men with a pump-sucker, who reported that "the water was tinged yellow—by eight tin cans in a state of decomposition. It had not been cleaned for twenty years before."[9]

One wonders what effect the tainted water can have wrought upon the constitutions of this all too susceptible family.

In January, Anne wrote demurely to Ellen Nussey:

> I am not going to give you 'a nice *long* letter'—on the contrary, I mean to content myself with a shabby little note, to be engulped in a letter of Charlotte's, which will, of course, be infinitely more acceptable to you than any production of mine, though I do not question your friendly regard for me, or the indulgent welcome you would accord to a missive of mine even without a more agreeable companion to back it, but you must know there is a lamentable deficiency in my organ of language, which makes me almost as bad a hand at writing as talking unless I have something particular to say. I have now, however, to thank you and your friend Miss Ringrose for your kind letter and her pretty watch-guards, which I am sure we shall all of us value the more for being the work of her own hands—You do not tell us how *you* bear the present unfavourable weather. We are all cut up by this cruel east wind, most of us, i.e. Charlotte, Emily, and I have had the influenza, or a bad cold instead, twice over within the space of a few weeks. Papa has had it once. Tabby has escaped it altogether. I have no news to tell you, for we have been nowhere, seen no one, and done nothing (to speak of) since you were here—and yet we contrive to be busy from morning to night.[10]

The letter, strictly truthful because the Brontës *were* doing "nothing to speak of", is slyly amusing.

Yet Ellen Nussey was not thrown completely off the scent. She had seen Charlotte correcting proofs of *Jane Eyre* and when the question of Currer Bell's identity arose, was shrewd enough to put two and two together.

The locality of "Lowood School" had been easily recognized as that of Cowan Bridge, and some indignation excited by Charlotte's description of the privations there. She later told Mrs Gaskell that she would not have written what she did if she had realized the place would be so readily identified. It is fairly certain that Ellen also identified the school and the character of Helen Burns from Charlotte's frequent descriptions of the place. In any event, she wrote to Charlotte, to ask if her friend had published any books.

The secret had already been confided to Mary Taylor, now at a safe distance in New Zealand. But Ellen was not completely in Charlotte's confidence. She was dearly loved but never completely trusted. Charlotte knew her friend's limitations, and while she wrote to Ellen with apparent frankness, kept secret vital portions of her own life. Perhaps she might have told Ellen sooner of her writing activities, but the tactful Ellen so far forgot herself as to ask outright. This was an invasion of privacy which could not be tolerated.

Dear Ellen,
All I can say to you about a certain matter is this; the report—if report there be—and if the lady, who seems to have been rather mystified, had not dreamt what she fancied had been told to her—must have had its origin in some absurd misunderstanding. I have given *no one* a right either to affirm, or hint, in the most distant manner that I am "publishing" (humbug!). Whoever has said it—if any one has, which I doubt—is no friend of mine. Though twenty books were ascribed to me, I should own none. I scout the idea utterly. Whoever, after I have distinctly rejected the charge, urges it upon me, will do an unkind and an ill-bred thing. The most profound obscurity is infinitely preferable to vulgar notoriety; and that notoriety I neither seek nor will have. If then any Birstallian or Gomersallian should presume to bore you on the subject—to ask you what "novel" Miss Brontë has been "publishing"—you can just say, with the distinct firmness of which you are perfectly mistress, when you choose, that you are authorized by Miss Brontë to say, that she repels and disowns every accusation of this kind. You may add, if you please, that if anyone has her confidence, you believe you have, and she has made no drivelling confessions to you on the subject.[11]

Long before, Miss Wooler had made the grave mistake of criticizing one Brontë to another Brontë. She had been reduced to tears by Charlotte's fury and excluded from friendship for some months. Now Ellen Nussey had invaded Charlotte's privacy, trespassing where friendship was no password. Henceforth, she must not concern herself with such matters. The relationship was to be conducted on Charlotte's terms, and those terms precluded Ellen's entering into that world where Currer Bell, famous novelist, took precedence over Charlotte Brontë.

NOTES TO CHAPTER SIXTEEN

1. Letter from Charlotte Brontë to W. S. Williams, 10th November 1847.
2. George Moore, *Conversations in Ebury Street* (Heinemann).
3. Charlotte Brontë, Biographical Notice of Ellis and Acton Bell.
4. Letter from Charlotte Brontë to W. S. Williams.
5. Letter from Charlotte Brontë to G. H. Lewes.
6. Charlotte Brontë, *Jane Eyre*, Chapter 38.
7. Letter from Charlotte Brontë to W. S. Williams.
8. Letter from Branwell Brontë to J. F. Leyland, January 1848.
9. Entry in Mr Brontë's private notebook.
10. Letter from Anne Brontë to Ellen Nussey, 4th January 1848.
11. Letter from Charlotte Brontë to Ellen Nussey, May 1848.

SEVENTEEN

The Tenant of Wildfell Hall

On 22nd June 1848, Charlotte wrote to W. S. Williams:

You will perhaps have observed that Mr Newby has announced a new work by Acton Bell. The advertisement has, as usual, a certain tricky turn to its working which I do not admire.[1]

"Tricky" is a beautifully apt description for Mr Newby. He had developed the art of innuendo to a surpassing degree. *The Tenant of Wildfell Hall*, by Acton Bell, was printed in July 1848. Opposite the title page, he printed some opinions of the Press on "Mr Bell's First Novel". The extracts were actually from reviews of *Wuthering Heights* and included such sentences as, "*Jane Eyre* it will be reflected was edited by Mr Currer Bell. Here are two tales so nearly related to *Jane Eyre* in cast of thought, incident, and language as to excite curiosity. All these might be the work of one hand." (*Atheneum*.) "The work has affinity to *Jane Eyre*." (*Spectator*.) "The work is strongly original. It reminds us of *Jane Eyre*." (*Britannia*.)

Mr Newby was not content with innuendo. In those pre-copyright days, a publisher might sell a manuscript abroad and the author would receive nothing. *The Tenant of Wildfell Hall* was sold to an American firm, on the understanding that it was actually the work of Currer Bell. Understandably, Messrs Smith and Elder wrote immediately to "Currer Bell" demanding an explanation.

Charlotte was horrified at the notion that she was suspected of double dealing. It was, at last, necessary for the "Bells" to reveal their identity.

On the day that the letter arrived, Charlotte and Anne packed a small suitcase. They walked through a snowstorm to Keighley, got to Leeds where they caught a train to London, arriving in the capital at eight o'clock the following morning. They went straight to the Chapter Coffee House in Paernoster Row, where Charlotte and Emily had stayed with their father, on the way to Brussels. Here they ordered breakfast, tidied themselves, then set off for 65 Cornhill, where the offices of Messrs Smith and Elder were situated.

Mr George Smith was working in his office, when two ladies requested an audience, firmly declining to give their names. Somewhat annoyed at the interruption, Mr Smith ordered them to be admitted. Two plainly-dressed women were shown in. The smaller of the two who wore spectacles handed him a letter addressed to Currer Bell, Esq. When asked where she had obtained it, Charlotte burst out laughing.

Both were highly delighted at the surprise they were able to spring. Explanations were gone into, and Mr Williams was summoned to the office to meet the "gentleman" with whom he was carrying on such a voluminous correspondence.

That evening, Mr Smith brought his two sisters and Mr Williams to the Coffee House from where a bewildered Charlotte and Anne were rushed to the Opera. Neither of the Brontës possessed low-necked evening dresses, but they swallowed their pride and went, without protesting, to a performance of Rossini's *Barber of Seville*.

Charlotte was so awed by the splendid red and gold décor of the Opera House that she could not resist nudging Mr Williams and confiding: "You know, I am not accustomed to this sort of thing."

The following morning, Mr Williams accompanied them to church. He was the ideal companion for the Brontës—a mild, middle-aged gentleman whose keen intellect was masked by a speech defect. Charlotte's natural kindness was aroused, and she took such pains to put him at his ease that she forgot her own shyness.

In the afternoon, Mr Smith took them to his mother's house

in Bayswater to dine. Although only the family were present, neither Charlotte nor Anne could relish a mouthful of the fine food placed before them.

On the Monday morning, they visited the Royal Academy, and the National Gallery. One wonders if the spectre of Branwell's old ambitions arose to haunt their thoughts as they toured the Exhibition. Once their brother had dreamed of having his paintings hung on these same walls. But the chance had been and gone. Branwell's sun was setting—Charlotte and Anne were in the morning of their success.

They dined again at Mr Smith's and had tea with Mr Williams, who proudly introduced them to his eight children. A daughter of Leigh Hunt's was there and sang some Tuscan folk songs.

On Tuesday morning, the sisters reboarded the train to Leeds, armed with books for Martha and Tabby, and a volume of Tennyson's Poems, presumably for Emily. In the middle of all the gaiety, they had found time to call upon Mr Newby to confront him with a physical denial of his statements and to extract an apology.[2]

Their identity was not entirely revealed. Although their publishers were now fully cognizant of it, they had been introduced everywhere as the "Misses Brown", and were dismissed as frumpish countrywomen.

Mr Smith declared later that Charlotte struck him as looking interesting, rather than attractive. Her friendship with the young, good-looking publisher was to ripen over the years and lead him to the conclusion that she would have given all her fame and all her genius to be beautiful. He was more favourably impressed by Anne, whom he described as "by no means pretty, yet of a pleasing appearance—Her manner was curiously expressive of a wish for protection and encouragement, a kind of constant appeal, which invited sympathy".

The visit to London had pleased Anne enormously, but Charlotte paid for her own excitement with a severe attack of migraine. She was, also, roundly scolded by Emily for having let slip the fact that they were *three* sisters. Emily obviously considered the trip to London an entire waste of time and was extremely annoyed to find herself even indirectly involved.[3]

The Tenant of Wildfell Hall was already a success. This novel,

which has suffered an eclipse during our own time, was in
1848 a best seller. Unfortunately the critics attacked it
violently, declaring that it had been written with the intention
of shocking the public.

Those who have seen Anne Brontë only through Charlotte's
eyes are in for a rude awakening when they read *The Tenant
of Wildfell Hall*. This is no gentle, pastoral story, but a brutally
realistic picture of a beautiful, wilful girl tied by matrimony to
an alcoholic. Anne had deliberately set out to write a didactic
novel against intemperance. In Charlotte's own words:

> The motives which dictated this choice were pure, but, I think,
> slightly morbid. She had, in the course of her life, been called on
> to contemplate, near at hand, and for a long time, the terrible
> effects of talents misused and faculties abused; hers was naturally
> a sensitive, reserved, and dejected nature; what she saw sank
> very deeply into her mind; it did her harm. She brooded over
> it till she believed it to be a duty to reproduce every detail (of
> course with fictitious characters, incidents, and situations) as a
> warning to others.[4]

Anne certainly intended her novel to serve as a moral warning, and being acquainted with the effects of alcohol at first
hand, was well able to describe the degradation that such
excesses could produce. It took courage to pursue such a task,
but to affirm that it shortened her life is Charlotte's exaggeration.

Work of any kind would have further weakened Anne's
precarious health, but there is absolutely no evidence to support
the theory that Anne's disease was intensified by the nature of
the work she had undertaken. She certainly considered it her
duty to point out the dangers of moral laxity, for in her Preface
to the second edition, she stated:

> Such humble talents as God has given me I will endeavour to
> put to their greatest use; if I am able to amuse, I will try to
> benefit too; and when I feel it my duty to speak an unpalatable
> truth, with the help of God, I *will* speak it, though it be to the
> prejudice of my name and to the detriment of my reader's imme-
> diate pleasure as well as my own.[5]

The Tenant of Wildfell Hall has been assumed by most
biographers to be an accurate representation of life at Thorp

Green. To assume this is surely to underestimate the power of Anne's imagination. She was not capable, as Emily was, of creating a world out of her own being, but she was perfectly able to reconstruct a society not as it actually was, but as it dramatically was.

Anne's picture of a dissolute, rakish household was merely the artistic frame into which she could fit her characters. Her style, however, was so blunt that what she had intended for a stage setting was thought to be a real description of places she had seen.

Similarly, her portrayal of Arthur Huntingdon was taken to be a representation of Branwell. Certainly, Anne lived close to one in whom drunkenness had become a way of life. She knew that vice is not always titanic, but becomes a petty, shabby thing. Yet Huntingdon bears no resemblance in character to Branwell. They are alike only in their habit of drinking. Anne was well aware that Branwell had a better side to his nature. Huntingdon is never credited with one. From first to last, he is a moral Caliban, who dies unrepentant. In attempting to portray the evils of intemperance, Anne displayed only one side of the coin. She weakened her novel by over-emphasis, which may explain its eclipse in recent years.

During the summer of 1848, both Emily and Anne were writing, steadily, carrying their desks out into the gardens where the currant bushes bloomed.[6]

There was no such peaceful haven for Mr Brontë and his son. On 22nd July, the parson received a letter from the landlord of the 'Old Cock', threatening to proceed to a summons if Branwell did not immediately discharge his debts. Mr Brontë, obviously unaware of their extent, gave his son ten shillings to cover them. Branwell, who was waiting for money from Dr Crosby, immediately appealed to Leyland, who, despite having pressing financial difficulties of his own, readily stood surety for his friend.[7]

Grundy wrote of a meeting that he had with Branwell during this period. He declared, probably inaccurately, that the meeting took place only two days before Branwell's death. Other biographers have declared it took place two years before, but the tone of the encounter, and his description of Branwell's appearance and state of mind, seem to place it somewhere in the summer of 1848.

Grundy had invited Branwell to dine with him at the 'Black Bull', but after waiting a while, he was surprised to see Mr Brontë, who came to apologize for his son's tardiness. Mr Brontë was certainly no devotee of the 'Black Bull', nor can he have possessed much in common with Grundy, but his perfect courtesy would preclude his condoning the discomfort of an acquaintance.

Branwell, who had been confined to bed for some days as a result of his excesses, was announced.

Presently the door opened cautiously and a head appeared. It was a mass of red unkempt, uncut hair, wildly floating round a great, gaunt forehead; the cheeks yellow and hollow, the mouth fallen, the thin lips not trembling but shaking, the sunken eyes once small, now glaring with the light of madness—I hastened to my friend, greeted him with my gayest manner, as I knew he liked best, drew him quickly into the room and forced on him a stiff glass of hot brandy. Under its influence, and that of the bright cheerful surroundings, he looked frightened, frightened of himself. He glanced at me for a moment, and muttered something of leaving a warm bed to come out into the cold night. Another glass of brandy and returning warmth gradually brought him back to something like the Brontë of old. He even ate something like the Brontë of old. He even ate some dinner, a thing he said he had not done for long; I never knew his intellect clearer. He described himself as waiting anxiously for death— indeed, longing for it, and happy, in these his sane moments, to think that it was so near. He once again declared that death would be due to the story I knew, and to nothing else.

When I was at last compelled to leave, he quietly drew from his sleeve a carving knife, placed it on the table and holding me by both hands, said that having given up all thoughts of seeing me again, he imagined when my letter came it was a call from Satin. Dressing himself, he took the knife, which he had long secreted, and came to the inn, with a firm determination to rush into the room and stab the occupant. In the excited state of his mind he did not recognize me when he opened the door, by my voice and manner conquered him, and "brought him home to himself". I left him standing bareheaded in the road, with bowed form and drooping tears.[8]

Branwell's periods of lucidity were growing shorter and occurring seldom. When he was well enough to rise, he went down to the 'Black Bull' where he could occupy his favourite armchair and drink deeply of the gin which Annie, the barmaid, served him.

If ever he glanced through the windows, he would see the high houses of the main street blocking the skyline, reminding him that he who had struggled against his environment all his life was now trapped by his own foolishness in the moorland village where his secret world began and ended.

To John, his old friend, he scrawled:

> I shall feel very much obliged to you if you can contrive to get me Fivepence worth of Gin in a proper measure. Should it be speedily got I could perhaps take it from you or Billy at the lane top, or, what would be quite as well, sent out for, to you.
> I anxiously ask the favour because I know the good it will do me.
> *Punctually* at Half-past Nine in the morning you will be paid the 5d. out of a shilling given me then.[9]

Only gin, or a dose of laudanum, would buy him a measure of oblivion. But their effect was wearing thin and could hold at bay the nightmare of reality for a limited space.

On 22nd September, Branwell went down into the village, probably to the Post Office, where money from Dr Crosby might be waiting. William Brown, brother of the sexton, met him halfway up the lane "panting for breath and unable to proceed". Brown helped him up to the door of the Parsonage and left him there.

For the remaining two days of his life, Branwell was confined to bed in the quiet room which he and his father had shared for some years. From this room, he had staggered forth to boast to his sisters that he and the "old man" had had a "terrible night of it". It was in this room that Mrs Brontë had died, gasping with her last breath, "Oh, God, my children! My poor children!"[10] Now Branwell lay there alone, with the ticking of the grandfather clock on the landing to mark the speedy passing of his time. That his constitution was shattered, Charlotte had remarked months previously,[11] but neither he nor the doctor considered the end to be so near.

Only the sudden easing of Branwell's restless spirit betokened that the strange calm which often heralds death had descended. He became again the boy they had adored.

In the last hours of his life, Branwell shed the cynical atheism which had broken his father's heart, and eagerly embraced the simple creed he had learned at Maria's knee.

Yet although life had failed him, death still held its terrors. John Brown was sitting with him, when Branwell seized his hand, and cried: "Oh, John, I'm dying!"

A few moments later, as the last agony began, Branwell moaned: "In all my life, I have done nothing great or good."

Twenty minutes later, after whispering "Amen" to a prayer of his father's Branwell was dead.

John Brown, after summoning the family, went out on to the steps of the Parsonage and stood, listening to the church bells as they called the villagers to worship.[12]

Chief Genius Branii, alias Percy Northangerland, alias Patrick Benjamin Higgins, alias Young Soult, went out of the world to the sound of bells—the same bells that Branwell, as a child, had loved to hear on Christmas morning, when he lay snugly in Maria's bed, and never thought of the future.

Branwell had ruined his own life, squandered his genius, alienated his sisters, and humiliated his father—yet nobody could have been more greatly mourned.

Grundy wrote perhaps the finest epitaph on his friend:

Patrick Branwell Brontë was no domestic demon; he was just a man moving in a mist who lost his way.[13]

NOTES TO CHAPTER SEVENTEEN

1. Letter from Charlotte Brontë to W. S. Williams, 22nd June 1848.
2. See letter from Charlotte Brontë to Mary Taylor. See also Mrs Gaskell, *The Life of Charlotte Brontë*.
3. Charlotte wrote to her publishers, asking them to forget her slip of the tongue.
4. Charlotte Brontë, Biographical Notice of Ellis and Acton Bell.
5. Anne Brontë, *The Tenant of Wildfell Hall*, Preface to the Second Edition.
6. Martha Brown, *Reminiscence of the Brontës*.

7. Letter from Branwell Brontë to J. F. Leyland.
8. F. A. Grundy, *Pictures of the Past*.
9. Letter from Branwell Brontë to John Brown.
10. Recounted by Mrs Wainwright to Mrs Gaskell.
11. Letter from Charlotte Brontë to Ellen Nussey.
12. Recounted by John Brown.
13. F. A. Grundy, *Pictures of the Past*.

EIGHTEEN

Sweet is Rest

Branwell had been of little practical use to his family while he was living, but his death severed the thread of their existence.

Genius sometimes comes to its height during periods of great tension. The domestic misfortunes of the Brontë sisters coincided, perhaps not accidentally, with the full flowering of their talents. It is a matter of speculation whether, if Branwell had made a success of his life, his sisters would have been driven to the refuge of their secret worlds—not as childish games of escape, but as breeding grounds for novels of genius.

Mr Brontë had broken down completely when his son died, for the loss of this beloved and brilliant child meant more to him than the loss of any of his daughters. Mr Brontë has been blamed for over-indulgence towards Branwell, but nobody can accuse him of indifference. No matter what his sins, Branwell never found the door of the Parsonage closed against him.

If Mr Brontë's loss was great, Charlotte's was even greater. Added to the grief at the loss of an only brother was an overwhelming sense of guilt at having been the one to cast him off. There is no evidence to support the theory that a reconciliation took place between Charlotte and her brother. If such a scene had occurred, Charlotte would surely have derived some comfort from the fact. As it was, she collapsed completely and was too ill to go to the funeral. Anne remained at home to nurse her sister. Emily accompanied her brother to his last resting place and watched the coffin being lowered into the vault where Maria and Elizabeth already slept.

The dramatic suddenness of Branwell's death following upon so notorious a life excited popular imagination. It was rumoured that Branwell had died on his feet and that his pockets were full of letters from Mrs Robinson.[1] Martha Brown explicitly denied that any correspondence was ever found and added staunchly that Branwell "was never as bad as he was made out to be".[2]

The Parson's son had always been a popular figure in Haworth. More than any other member of the family, he had entered into the life of the village. Oddly, the frequent failures and scandals of his short life had not resulted in his being ostracized. "T'parson's Pat" went to his grave in the midst of a violent thunderstorm—a circumstance which would have delighted his Gothic spirit. It was in this torrential rain that Emily is said to have caught the severe cold which led to her death.

Emily herself ignored her ailments. She had suffered constantly from colds and chills during the previous year, and her handwriting is noticeably uneven from July 1848 onwards, but the more dramatic decline in the health of her brother and Anne's constant delicacy, led to an overlooking of her condition by the family which, no doubt, she welcomed. The thoughts of all of them still centred, naturally enough, upon Branwell's death.

A fortnight after Branwell's death, Charlotte wrote to W. S. Williams.

> When I looked on the noble face and forehead of my dead brother (Nature had favoured him with a fairer outside, as well as a finer constitution than his sisters) and asked myself what had made him go ever wrong, tend ever downwards, when he had so many gifts to induce to, and aid, in an upward course, I seemed to receive an oppressive revelation of the feebleness of humanity; of the inadequacy of even genius to lead to true greatness, if unaided by religion and principle.[3]

Even while racked by her own conscience, Charlotte must needs shift the blame. She declared that the loss of Branwell's

K

religious principles had led to his downfall. Rather should she have said that his atheism was the *result* of his downfall because, having failed to aspire to Maria's Paradise, he preferred to disbelieve in its existence rather than be excluded from its joys.

Branwell's death was stated to be due to "bronchitis and marasmus"[4]—wasting of the flesh—but it is difficult at this stage to pinpoint the actual disease which caused his death. His constitution was ruined by alcohol and opium; he had suffered all his life from insomnia and fits and it is almost certain that he was consumptive.

Various last-minute remedies had obviously been tried and equally clearly had failed; Emily's refusal to allow "any poisoning doctor" near her may have stemmed in part from a belief, mistaken or otherwise, that such remedies had aggravated Branwell's condition rather than relieved it.

Peace had returned to the household. The sisters could write openly, with no fear of Branwell discovering their work and Mr Brontë could sleep soundly in his bed.

But it was an uneasy peace. Charlotte, who was writing *Shirley*—a novel chosen with great care as to subject and setting —found the work grew very slowly. To W. S. Williams, she confided:

> Emily's cold and cough are very obstinate. I fear she has pain in her chest, and I sometimes catch a shortness in her breathing when she has moved at all quickly. She looks very thin and pale. Her reserved nature occasions me great uneasiness of mind. It is useless to question her; you get no answers. It it still more useless to recommend remedies, they are never adopted.[5]

Much has been written of Emily's attitude towards death. The physical decay of a mortal body held no terrors for her. So far as one can judge, physical attributes disgusted her. Emily had experienced the sensation of being "out of the body", and knew the agony with which the soul returned to its fleshy prison.

That Emily should fail after Branwell's funeral is dramatically perfect. She, the strongest in the household, had cared for her brother during his decline. Constant strain will affect the hardest constitutions and Emily was, despite outward appearances, not a hardy person. Sheer strength of will must have kept her on her feet and, when Branwell died, her practical use on earth must have seemed to her to be at an end.

Emily looked forward eagerly to death, wrapped in a strange isolation which Anne and Charlotte dared not invade.

Although Emily's cough and increasing weakness kept her indoors, she refused to lie in bed or even rest. It was so bitterly cold that she reluctantly allowed Mr Nicholls to exercise the dogs, but every other regular task was performed as before.

Offers of help were met with silence or contempt. Emily rose at seven in the morning and retired at ten in the evening, moving slowly about her work although her breathing could be heard all over the house, and a gust of wind from the open door sent her reeling against the wall.

When Dr Wheelhouse, who had attended Branwell, was called in, Emily locked herself in her bedroom. Although the doctor left some medicine she refused to touch it.

In desperation, Charlotte wrote to a homœopathic physician, giving details of her sister's condition.

Her appetite failed; she evinced a constant thirst, with a craving for acids, and required a constant change of beverage. In appearance she grew rapidly emaciated, her pulse—the only time she allowed it to be felt—was found to be 115 per minute. The patient usually appeared worse in the forenoon, she was then frequently exhausted and drowsy; towards evening she often seemed better. Expectoration accompanies the cough. The shortness of breath is aggravated by the slightest exertion. The patient's sleep is supposed to be tolerably good at intervals, but disturbed by paroxysms of coughing.

It was too late for medical advice even if Emily could have been persuaded to take it. Even the re-issue of their original book of poetry failed to elicit any response. The *Poems*, issued this time by Messrs Smith and Elder, caused little excitement among the critics or public.

Charlotte wrote bitterly:

I should have thought more of them had they more fully recognized Ellis Bell's merits; but the lovers of abstract poetry are few in number.[6]

Emily's own comment was a scornful smile, but her indifference was merely assumed. After her death, several hostile reviews of her novel and of her poems were found, cut out and hidden within her desk.

To write now was impossible, for she could scarcely read, but this did not prevent Mr Newby from announcing that he hoped, shortly, to bring before the public, new novels by Ellis and Acton Bell.

Charlotte wrote angrily :

> Ellis is at present in no condition to trouble himself with the thoughts of writing or publishing. Should it please Heaven to restore his health and strength, he reserves to himself the right of deciding whether or not Mr Newby has forfeited every claim to his second work.[7]

A visit from Mrs Robinson's daughters was a welcome diversion. Charlotte thought them attractive, stylish girls and was deeply touched by their evident devotion to Anne. Mrs Robinson had now married Sir Edward Scott—a final humiliation which Branwell, by his death, had avoided.

After the visit, the routine of the Parsonage continued. Neither Emily nor Anne could venture out of doors and Charlotte, locked by love and duty in the cold, grey house, found her only pleasure in the parcels of books which Mr Williams was sending to her.

Neither pain nor pleasure could penetrate to Emily's consciousness now. After a long search over the barren hills, Charlotte found a sprig of heather and took it into her sister, but Emily could not even recognize her favourite flowers.[8]

On 19th December, Charlotte wrote to Ellen :

> I should have written to you before, if I had had one word of hope to say; but I have not. She grows daily weaker. The physician's opinion was expressed too obscurely to be of use. He sent some medicine, which she would not take. Moments so dark as these I have never known. I pray for God's support to us all. Hitherto he has granted it.[9]

By noon, Emily could speak only in gasps. Her last recorded words were : "If you will send for the doctor, I will see him now."

About two o'clock Emily died, fully-dressed, leaning against the old horsehair sofa in the sitting-room. One wonders whether her last request was a bid to ease the minds of her sisters, or a sudden panic as the imminent separation of soul and body became an agony too great to bear. Did she suddenly realize, as Catherine Earnshaw had done, that even in Heaven she would be homesick for the moors?

Charlotte wrote to Ellen:

Emily suffers no more from pain or weakness now. She never will suffer more in this world. She is gone, after a hard, short conflict. She died on Tuesday, the very day I wrote to you. I thought it very possible she might be with us still for weeks; and a few hours afterwards she was in eternity. Yes; there is no Emily in time or on earth now. Yesterday, we put her poor, wasted, mortal frame quietly under the church pavement. We are very calm at present. Why should we be otherwise? The anguish of seeing her suffer is over, the spectacle of the pains of death is gone by; the funeral day is past. We feel she is at peace. No need to tremble for the hard frost and the keen wind. Emily does not feel them. She died in a time of promise. We saw her taken from life in its prime. But it is God's will, and the place where she is gone is better than that she has left.[10]

Emily's death made little stir in the village. She died as she had lived, solitary and independent. Few people were aware that she had ever written a word.

Keeper, her dog, joined the small procession through the lych-gate, and lay quietly in the church aisle while the burial service was being read. Then he came home, and, lying outside Emily's room, howled pitifully for the woman whose nature had been as intractable as his own.

Christmas was a quiet and mournful season, with ice and snow to prevent Ellen from paying a long-promised visit.

Charlotte wrote:

Some sad comfort I take as I hear the wind blow and feel the cutting keenness of the frost, in knowing the elements bring no more suffering—their severity cannot reach her grave—her fever is quieted, her restlessness soothed, her deep, hollow cough is hushed for ever—My father says to me, almost hourly, "Charlotte, you must bear up—I shall sink if you fail me"—The sight too of my sister Anne's very still but deep sorrow wakens in me such fear for her that I dare not falter. Somebody *must* cheer the rest.

So I will not now ask why Emily was torn from us in the

fulness of our attachment, rooted up in the prime of her own days, in the promise of her powers—why her existence now lies like a field of green corn trodden down—like a tree in full bearing, struck at the root. I will only say, sweet is rest after labour, and repeat again and again that Emily knows that now.[11]

NOTES TO CHAPTER EIGHTEEN

1. Mrs Gaskell, *Life of Charlotte Brontë*.
2. Clement Shorter, *The Brontë Circle*.
3. Letter from Charlotte Brontë to W. S. Williams, 6th October . 1848.
4. Branwell Brontë's Death Certificate in Haworth Parsonage Museum.
5. Letter from Charlotte Brontë to W. S. Williams, 29th October, 1848.
6. Letter from Charlotte Brontë to W. S. Williams.
7. Letter from Charlotte Brontë to W. S. Williams.
8. Mrs Gaskell, *Life of Charlotte Brontë*.
9. Letter from Charlotte Brontë to Ellen Nussey, 18th December 1848.
10. Letter from Charlotte Brontë to Ellen Nussey, 21st December 1848.
11. Letter from Charlotte Brontë to W. S. Williams, 25th December 1848.

NINETEEN

Take Courage, Charlotte

The person most affected by Emily's death was her younger sister, Anne. It is no exaggeration to say that, without Emily, Anne was incapable of living for any length of time. Ellen Nussey had said they were like twins, inseparable, as Charlotte and Branwell had once been.

Emily had been the leader of the two, but if any softening influence ever mitigated the harshness of her nature, then surely it was exerted by Anne. Emily had achieved heights of spiritual experience to which Anne could not attain, but both sisters shared Gondal, "playing" at it when both were grown to maturity.

Charlotte loved Anne but obviously considered her talents to be slight. Emily would not, I feel, have made that mistake. Anne was admitted into Emily's confidence to a far greater extent than Charlotte ever was, and sentiment alone could not have dictated Emily's choice of companion.

The light-hearted, attractive girl had struggled all her life against ill-health and excessive shyness. Her natural gaiety had been subdued by the Calvinistic tenets drummed into her by Aunt Branwell, by the death of William Weightman and the disgrace of her brother. Throughout these trials she had always had the companionship of Emily in whom she probably confided.

Now Emily was dead and from the day of her funeral, Anne

noticeably drooped and sickened. Charlotte turned, heavy-hearted, from the writing of her novel to the more important task of nursing her last sister.

At the beginning of January, a specialist from Leeds was called in to examine her and confirmed what the family already suspected. Both lungs were affected by tuberculosis. Life might be prolonged, but not saved.

Ellen Nussey was paying the long-awaited visit when the specialist came, and she described Anne as "looking sweetly pretty and in capital spirits for an invalid". Consumption is a flattering disease and Anne's delicate skin was evidently so flushed with fever that she gave the superficial impression of health.

When the physical examination was concluded, the specialist went with Mr Brontë into the study, while Anne remained in the sitting-room with her sister and her friend. According to Ellen Nussey, Anne chattered in a very lively fashion. Eventually, Mr Brontë came in, sat down on the sofa, and drawing his daughter towards him, said: "My *dear* little Anne."[1]

It was Anne's death sentence and, although outwardly, she accepted it with the same patient fortitude she had taken over other misfortunes, the poem she began two days later expresses her real feelings.

> A dreadful darkness closes in
> On my bewildered mind;
> O let me suffer, and not sin,
> Be tortured, yet resigned.

The words reveals such an intensity of suffering that Charlotte omitted them from her edited version of Anne's poetry. In the published poems, the lines begin:

> I hoped amid the brave and strong
> My portioned task might lie,
> To toil amid the labouring throng
> With purpose keen and high;
> But Thou hast fixed another part,
> And Thou hast fixed it well,
> I said so with my bleeding heart
> When first the anguish fell.

Charlotte could understand the resignation of her sister's nature, but the lonely struggle which led to such quiet acceptance could not be borne. Deeply as she loved her younger sister, Charlotte never guessed the mental and spiritual torments she was enduring. When she discovered Anne's poems after her death, she was horrified at their naked misery and probably felt guilty because she had lacked the perception to see that Anne had passed through such a crisis alone.

While Anne fought silently with her fear of death, and with the crushing disappointment of leaving the world before she had accomplished any great good, Charlotte was writing to Ellen, "Her mind seems generally serene, and her sufferings hitherto are nothing like Emily's".[2]

The progress of the disease was slower and less painful than Emily's had been, but it was none the less inexorable. Anne's docility was such that she readily submitted to the nauseous remedies prescribed during that era and Charlotte derived some comfort from discussing with her sister the efficacy of various medicines.

Anne was not the only invalid in the Parsonage. Mr Brontë, whose health had long been considered delicate, suffered badly from rheumatism and bronchitis during the long winter and Charlotte herself had an alarming cough and severe chest pains, which she tried to relieve by the application of mustard and vinegar poultices.

It was with relief that Charlotte could write to W. S. Williams, at the beginning of March:

My sister still continues better, she has less languor and weakness; her spirits are improved. This change gives cause, I think, both for gratitude and hope.

The change was but a temporary respite. By April, the old symptoms had returned. Charlotte wrote for advice to Dr Forbes, a lung specialist, who told Anne to take cod-liver oil, a remedy which made her sick and diminished her already minute appetite.

The doctors had recommended a change of air, and Anne yearned towards the sea. She had a great fancy for Scarborough, where she had spent some of her happiest times. She felt also that Charlotte's own health might be revived by different

surroundings. Unfortunately, Mr Brontë objected strongly to
being left alone, with only the two servants to minister to him.
When the weather was milder, he thought he might manage,
but in the meantime, he considered it to be Charlotte's duty
to remain at home.

Charlotte was thrown between two stools, with filial duty
and sisterly affection on opposite sides. She could not defy her
father's command, yet she longed to gratify her sister's
wishes.

Anne finally took the unusual step of writing to Ellen Nussey,
to ask if Miss Nussey would be willing to accompany her to
Scarborough, either with or without Charlotte.

> The doctors say that change of air or removal to a better
> climate would hardly ever fail of success in consumptive cases
> if the remedy were taken *in time*, but the reason why there are
> so many disappointments is, that it is deferred until it is too late.
> Now, I would not commit this error; and to say the truth, though
> I suffer much less from pain and fever than I did when you were
> with us, I am decidedly weaker and very much thinner, my
> cough still troubles me a good deal, especially in the night, and,
> what seems worse than all I am subject to great shortness of
> breath on going upstairs or any slight exertion. Under these
> circumstances I think there is no time to be lost. I have no horror
> of death; if I thought it inevitable I think I could quietly resign
> myself to the prospect, in the hope that you, dear Miss Nussey,
> would give as much of your company as you possibly could to
> Charlotte, and be a sister to her in my stead. But I wish it would
> please God to spare me not only for Papa's and Charlotte's sakes,
> but because I long to do some good in the world before I leave it.
> I have many schemes in my head for future practice—humble
> and limited indeed—but still I would not like to see them come
> to nothing, and myself to have lived to so little purpose.[3]

The letter so moved Ellen that she sent it to Charlotte, who
replied:

> I read Anne's letter to you; it was touching enough, as you
> say. If there were no hope beyond this world—no eternity, no
> life to come—Emily's fate, and that which threatens Anne,
> would be heart-breaking. I cannot forget Emily's death-day; it
> becomes a more fixed, a darker, a more frequently recurring
> idea in my mind than ever. It was very terrible. She was torn,

conscious, panting, reluctant, though resolute, out of a happy life. But it *will not* do to dwell on these things.[4]

Miss Wooler, to whom Charlotte had confided their hopes of going to Scarborough, offered them the use of her own house there. It was politely refused, for not only did the Brontës shrink from being placed under any unnecessary obligation, but Miss Wooler's house overlooked North Bay, at some distance from that part of the town which Anne had loved during her holidays with the Robinsons.

The Brontës booked rooms at Mrs Wood's Boarding House, on St Nicholas Cliff, overlooking the South Bay. Anne, with that seldom-fulfilled desire for gaiety which characterized her, thought the atmosphere of a boarding house would be more lively. Expense was, for once, considered of little importance. Three months before, Fanny Outhwaite, Anne's godmother from Thornton, had died and bequeathed Anne a legacy of two hundred pounds. The money, Charlotte decided, must be used in order to sweeten what remained of her sister's existence.

Mr Brontë, aware of his youngest daughter's determination, gave in gracefully over the matter of his own convenience and gave Charlotte the required permission to visit Scarborough with her sister. Ellen Nussey was to accompany them, for her relatives, although they objected to her being Anne's sole companion on the trip, were not averse to her completing a trio.

While Anne spoke hopefully of the possible benefits of a change of air, Charlotte wrote to Ellen.

It is with a heavy heart I prepare; and earnestly do I wish the fatigue of the journey were well over. It may be borne better than I expect, for temporary stimulus often does much; but when I see the daily increasing weakness, I know not what to think. I fear you will be shocked when you see Anne; but be on your guard, dear Ellen, not to express your feelings; indeed, I can trust both your self-possession and kindness.[5]

It was arranged that Ellen would meet the sisters at Leeds station, but on the appointed day Anne was too ill to leave home. There was no way of informing Ellen who consequently waited for several hours at the railway terminal. The following day, probably fearing that the worst had already happened, she travelled to Haworth just in time to see the invalid being lifted into the gig which was to take them to Keighley.

They stayed overnight at York where, at Anne's request, they visited the Minster. The soaring spires of the monument to the omnipotence of God had always stirred Anne's aesthetic sense; now the glory of it moved her to tears. She cried out, "If finite power can do this what is the—?" and was hastened away because her companions feared the effects of too much emotion. The following day, they reached their destination, fatigued by their long journey but cheered along the route by the kindness they met.

On 26th May, they went down on to the sands where Anne rode in a donkey cart and astonished the driver by taking over the reins and lecturing him severely for driving his animals too hard.

The next morning, Anne was anxious to go to church, but both Charlotte and Ellen dissuaded her from making the attempt.

In the afternoon they went for a walk, but Anne insisted that Charlotte and Ellen walk on ahead to enjoy the scenery already familiar to her. According to a lady staying at the Woods', Anne made her way home alone but fell down at the entrance gate and was distressed lest Charlotte or Ellen hear of the accident.

During the evening, having watched the sunset, the three discussed the possibility of Anne's dying while on holiday and the desire that she evinced to be buried in Scarborough, to spare her father the agony of burying yet another child.

Anne rose at seven o'clock as usual on 28th May and performed her own toilet before coming down into the breakfast room. About eleven o'clock she spoke of feeling a change and a doctor was immediately brought.

Previously unacquainted with the circumstances, he was considerably taken aback to discover his patient fully dressed, and seated in a chair by the window. When she asked him if there was time for her to reach home, he was forced to admit that she was already dying. She thanked him and promised to call him again, if it were necessary.

Emily had died at two o'clock and by a strange coincidence,

Anne also died at that hour. According to Ellen Nussey, she died
painlessly and calmly, with the final words, "Take courage,
Charlotte! Take courage!"

So unspectacular was her end that as Charlotte was closing
her dead sister's eyes, the landlady put her head round the door
to announce the arrival of dinner.[6]

For Charlotte, it came, despite the long months of hopeless
waiting, as a shock. She had longed for Anne to be released
from pain and dreaded the final loneliness when this, the most
pliable of her sisters, fell into her final sleep.

Charlotte and Ellen buried her high on the cliff, above the
beach where she had once hunted for sea-shells. They remained
at Scarborough together for almost a month and from Scarborough Charlotte penned her little note to Martha Brown in
which the simple, kindly phrases reveal an attractive side of
her nature. Tedious and sententious she might be at times, but
when occasion required she could descend, without patronage,
to the intellectual level of a servant.

> I am very much pleased with your note, and glad to learn
> that all at home are getting on pretty well. It will still be a week
> or ten days before I return, and you must not tire yourself too
> much with the cleaning.
> My sister Anne's death could not be otherwise than a great
> trouble to me, though I have known for many weeks that she
> could not get better. She died very calmly and gently; she was
> quite sensible to the last. About three minutes before she died
> she said she was very happy, and believed she was passing out
> of earth into heaven. It was not her custom to talk much about
> religion; but she was very good, and I am certain she is now in a
> far better place than this world contains.[7]

In July, Charlotte and Ellen parted company, the one to
return to her relatives, the other to go back to the place she
still described as home, likening it to the city of London after an
earthquake.

When Charlotte reached the Parsonage, the dogs ran out to
greet her, then sniffed about in search of Emily and Anne. Mr
Brontë welcomed her eagerly and she was touched by the care
with which Tabby and Martha had cleaned her room and
brightened everywhere. But there was now no companion with
whom to share her ambitions or her fears. She dare not com-

plain to her father, for his constant enquiries as to her health irritated and depressed her.

Only to Ellen did she reveal a glimpse of the soul-searing misery of her days.

Sometimes when I wake in the morning, and know that Solitude, Remembrance, and Longing are to be almost my sole companions all day through—that at night I shall go to bed with them, that they will keep me sleepless—that next morning I shall wake to them again—sometimes, Nell, I have a heavy heart of it. But crushed I am not, yet; nor robbed of elasticity, nor of hope, nor quite of endeavour. I have some strength to fight the battle of life— But I do hope and pray that never may you, or anyone I love, be placed as I am. To sit in a lonely room—the clock ticking loud through a still house—and have open before the mind's eye the record of the last year, with its shocks, sufferings, losses —is a trial.[8]

NOTES TO CHAPTER NINETEEN

1. Ellen Nussey's reminiscences.
2. Letter from Charlotte Brontë to Ellen Nussey, 1849.
3. Letter from Anne Brontë to Ellen Nussey, written so closely with its sentences crossing that at a casual glance it appears as a piece of embroidery.
4. Letter from Charlotte Brontë to Ellen Nussey.
5. Letter from Charlotte Brontë to Ellen Nussey.
6. Ellen Nussey wrote out an account of the death of Anne Brontë for Mrs Gaskell.
7. Letter from Charlotte Brontë to Martha Brown.
8. Letter from Charlotte Brontë to Ellen Nussey, 1849.

TWENTY

Shirley

Few people can ever have been placed in Charlotte's position. All her life the company of her family and a few friends had satisfied her social needs. Now her family, with the exception of her seventy-two year old father, were gone, and with Mary Taylor in New Zealand and Ellen seldom free to visit, she led an existence of almost intolerable solitude.

Mr Brontë's sight was again beginning to fail him and as Tabby was over eighty years old and lame, Charlotte was able to occupy herself during the day with housework or reading aloud. Her father allowed her to act as his secretary, but the habits of a life-time are not easily broken. He still ate his meals alone and retired early to bed. Charlotte sat alone in the sitting-room finishing the novel *Shirley*, begun when all four Brontës were alive.

Charlotte pursued her task diligently, writing not from inspiration but as a matter of discipline. When her hand grew tired, she walked slowly for an hour or more around the table, as she and her sisters had done when their writing was completed for the day.

Autumn came, bringing with it the constant "low fever" dreaded by all residents of Haworth. Martha fell seriously ill with the complaint, and Tabby, attempting to do a greater share of the housework, fell heavily in the kitchen. This was the straw that broke the camel's back. Charlotte lost control completely and wept bitterly, confessing later to Ellen that she had behaved like a fool.

Under these conditions, *Shirley* was finished and dispatched to the publishers. It was important that the book should do well not only because Charlotte wished to consolidate her reputation, but because the railway shares in which she and her sisters had invested the bulk of their aunt's legacy had dropped alarmingly in value.

Shirley was published on 26th October 1849 and received, as usual, a mixed reception from the critics. It is fashionable these days to belittle this second novel and, certainly, it lacks the power and the strong personal appeal of *Jane Eyre*. Most of *Jane Eyre* sprang from personal experience and unsatisfied desires. It was an intensely subjective work of art. For her second novel, Charlotte had searched carefully for a theme, and found it in the various stories of the Luddite riots—stories familiar to her since her schooldays at Roe Head.

The heroine of the novel is traditionally supposed to be a portrait of Emily. Certainly they share some external characteristics but *Shirley* is no more akin to Emily than 'Huntingdon' was to Branwell.

Charlotte was at her best when she dealt with overwhelming emotions among a small group of people. There are, however, so many characters in *Shirley* that the emotion tends to become dispersed and weakened. The book with its various interruptions occasioned by family misfortune is uneven in style and the sombre banality of its ending contrasts unfavourably with its lively, humorous beginning. But, for all that, it is an intensely readable story and many of the minor characters are drawn with skill and sympathy.

It was this very skill which led to the unmasking of her anonymity. So localized were the situations, and the dialect in which the book is partly written, that it was deduced the writer must be a native of Haworth. One gentleman, a former resident of the village, confirmed his suspicions to a Liverpool newspaper, adding a rider to the effect that he believed only Miss Brontë, daughter of the incumbent of Haworth, could have produced such a work.

Currer Bell's real identity was greeted locally with pleasure and surprise. Mr Nicholls, the curate, whom Charlotte had caricatured unmercifully, was delighted. His landlady heard him reading the relevant passages of *Shirley* aloud to himself, then slapping his leg and roaring with laughter.

While conjecture was becoming certainty, Charlotte was not, in fact, at home. She had gone down to London to consult a specialist, for her chronic cough and chest pains were all too reminiscent of the symptoms of tuberculosis. The specialist, however, pronounced her lungs to be sound, and greatly relieved by the verdict, Charlotte determined to enjoy her brief respite from the loneliness of Haworth.

Charlotte again stayed with the Smiths, where by unspoken consent her pseudonym was dropped. Her hosts, aware of her abnormal shyness, were anxious that she should enjoy herself and, with a view to pleasing her, invited Thackeray to call.

The thought of meeting her literary idol unnerved Charlotte to such an extent that she suffered a severe attack of migraine and felt stupidly clumsy during the ordeal of the dinner party. Thackeray teased her in the sophisticated way of a man of the world, but the teasing fell flat, for Charlotte innocently answered every remark at face value and then became covered with confusion when she observed the other guests smiling behind their hands.

A later meeting with Thackeray was equally unsuccessful. The author of *Vanity Fair* invited the author of *Jane Eyre* to dinner and all those present waited eagerly for a sparkling duel of wits. They were disappointed.

Charlotte fixed her eyes on her host and waited for the pearls of wisdom she expected to fall from his lips. Unfortunately, Thackeray was far too interested in carving the joint and conversation died away almost before it had begun. The relentless silence of his guest so discomposed Thackeray that he made some excuse to leave the room and, slipping through the back door, fled to the sanctuary of his club.

A more fortunate meeting took place with Harriet Martineau, to whom Charlotte had sent a copy of *Shirley*. Miss Martineau invited the author, whom she knew only as Currer Bell, to tea and awaited the arrival of her guest with some impatience. Finally, Miss Brontë was announced and came in, "in a deep mourning dress, neat as a Quaker's, with her beautiful hair

L

smooth and brown, her fine eyes blazing with meaning, and her sensible face indicating a habit of self-control".

Harriet Martineau, with her strong will, almost masculine intellect, and ascetic habits had some quality of Emily Brontë in her—the only explanation, I think, for the ease with which Charlotte was enabled to throw off her reserve and talk freely.[1]

It was easy, too, for Charlotte to converse with her publisher, George Smith; he was younger than she and would not, so she imagined, fall in love with her. His mother evidently held different views on the subject and George Smith admitted that she had displayed some uneasiness about the strength of his attachment to Charlotte Brontë.

Other members of the household found Charlotte to be a difficult companion. She had very little small talk and possessed none of the graces which attract at first glance. She was well aware of her deficiencies in this respect and remarked, sadly, that, if anybody looked by accident at her face, he took care not to glance in that corner of the room again.

While Charlotte was staying in London, *The Times* published a particularly scathing report of *Shirley*. Deeply wounded by the attack, Charlotte wept bitterly* No amount of social intercourse could provide her with less sensitive nerves or with a nature better able to withstand criticism.

One person who genuinely enjoyed Charlotte's visit to London was Mr Brontë. His daughter was now famous and, welcomed by the great, was enjoying the splendours of the metropolis.

In the past, Emily had joked it was a waste of time for her to go travelling, "because Charlotte will bring it all home to me".

Now Charlotte used her powers of description that her father might enjoy, vicariously, not only her social engagements, but the trips to the National Gallery, the Zoo and Prince Albert's Armoury, in which Mr Brontë, as befitted his martial leanings, had evinced a particular interest.

Charlotte returned to Haworth to find that the secret of her identity was out. Even Martha Brown knew that her mistress

---

* The Smiths tried, unsuccessfully, to hide the reviews.

had written "two of the grandest books that ever was seen", and informed Charlotte excitedly that the Mechanics' Institute intended to order three copies of each. Local excitement ran high and pleased Charlotte, although she affected to laugh at it.[2]

Charlotte's personal life continued as uneventfully as before. Duty to her father kept her at home, but she described it as a grey, gloomy place where the arrival of the postman was the only thing for which to look forward. Her nerves were bad—so bad that she confessed it was her habit to sit and listen for her sisters' voices calling to her above the howling of the wind. Her eyesight was troubling her, so she could neither read nor write for long periods, but confined herself to knitting and sat up, later and later, in the solitary sitting-room. Even an occasional walk on the moors failed to cheer her.

When I go out there alone everything reminds me of the time when others were with me and then the moors seem a wilderness, featureless, solitary, saddening. My sister Emily had a particular love for them, and there is not a knoll of heather, nor a branch of fern, not a young bilberry leaf, nor a fluttering lark or linnet, but reminds me of her. The distant prospects were Anne's delight, and when I look round she is in the blue tints, the pale mists, the waves and shadows of the horizon. In the hill-country their poetry comes by lines and stanzas into my mind; once I loved it; now I dare not read it.[3]

Charlotte's greatest pleasure lay in the parcels of books sent to her regularly from Cornhill. To W. S. Williams, gratefully, she wrote:

What, I sometimes ask, could I do without them? I have recourse to them as to friends; they shorten and cheer many an hour that would be too long and too desolate otherwise.[4]

Charlotte derived pleasure, too, from her correspondence with Miss Martineau and with G. H. Lewes, although her friendship with the latter suffered somewhat when Lewes wrote a review of *Shirley* in which he called particular attention to the sex of the author. Charlotte heartily disliked the convention which judged 'female' works at a different level than those written by men and Lewes' pseudo-gallant references to women writers called forth her famous note:

To G. H. Lewes, Esq.,
I can be on my guard against my enemies, but God deliver me
from my friends.
                Currer Bell.

Mr Brontë obtained almost as much delight from his daughter's literary correspondence as she did. Bereft of his other
children, he was overwhelmed by Charlotte's fame and insisted
that she describe to him over and over again the appearance,
manners and conversation of the great figures she had met in
London. He also showed his increasing confidence in her by
allowing her to read some letters written by Mrs Brontë to him
before their marriage. Charlotte thought them, "truly fine,
pure, and elevated—I wished that she had lived, and that I had
known her.[5]
Despite increasing fame, Charlotte's seclusion remained almost
uninterrupted. Casual calls at the Parsonage had never been
encouraged, and few strangers braved the icy roads and bleak
winds of the heights to catch a glimpse of Currer Bell. Among
those who did come were Sir James and Lady Kay-Shuttleworth.
They pressed Charlotte to visit them at Gawthorpe Hall, their
home on the east borders of Lancashire.
Charlotte went, reluctantly, because she was aware that it
appealed to the snobbish side of her father's nature and enjoyed
the visit more than she expected, for the Shuttleworth residence
was a stately, grey house of some antiquity, and her hosts,
wishing to please, took her for long drives in the heavily
wooded country. She returned home, after promising to accompany them to London, but an attack of bronchitis suffered by
Mr Brontë gave her an excuse to remain in Haworth.
Charlotte confessed to Ellen :

I cannot say that I regret having missed this ordeal; I would
as lief have walked among red-hot ploughshares, but I do regret
one great treat which I shall now miss. Next Wednesday is the
anniversary dinner of the Royal Literary Fund Society, held in
Freemasons' Hall. Octavian Blewitt, the secretary, offered me a
ticket for the ladies' gallery. I should have seen all the great
literati and artists gathered in the hall below, and heard them
speak; Thackeray and Dickens are always present among the rest.
This cannot now be. I don't think all London can afford another
sight to me so interesting.[6]

Charlotte eventually visited London at the beginning of June —not with the Shuttleworths who were detained by illness, but to stay quietly with the Smiths.

Charlotte and Thackeray met again, when she questioned him earnestly about his work and was deeply puzzled at the flippancy of his replies. She also met G. H. Lewes and was moved almost to tears by the strong facial resemblance he bore to Emily.[7] Perhaps her most exciting experience was a glimpse of the aged Duke of Wellington. All her life Wellington had been the arch-hero who had figured largely in their childhood games. It was the name she had bestowed upon the little wooden soldier given to her by Branwell. It was the name under which she had written many of her miniature newspapers and magazines. To see him must have been poignant indeed.

Charlotte interrupted her stay in London in order to visit Edinburgh with George Smith, who was called there by family matters. The Scottish expedition was looked on with no favourable eye by Mrs Smith Senior, but Charlotte fell in love with the granite city and enthused over its lofty beauties.

Charlotte returned home laden with a crayon drawing of herself by Richmond and a portrait of the Duke of Wellington as a gift for her father.[8] Mr Brontë admired both pictures, although he considered the artist might have flattered his daughter more. Tabby, however, declared that Charlotte's portrait looked "too old" and, her perceptions dulled by age, insisted that the portrait of Wellington was one of Mr Brontë.[9]

Charlotte might be amused at the incident, but it cannot have been all amusement for her with two old people constantly dependent upon her for care and companionship. When she was not tending to their needs, she roamed about on the moors or sat in the lonely sitting-room. Even the hearty Kay-Shuttleworths were preferable to this and Charlotte had been home for scarcely more than a fortnight, when she accepted an invitation from them to visit the Lake District.

Another guest had been invited to meet Charlotte and in the brightly-lit drawing room at the Briery, she and her future biographer came face to face with each other for the first time.

NOTES TO CHAPTER TWENTY

1. Miss Martineau gave Mrs Gaskell much useful information but disliked the finished biography.
2. Letter from Charlotte Brontë to Ellen Nussey.
3. Letter from Charlotte Brontë to W. S. Williams.
4. Letter from Charlotte Brontë to W. S. Williams.
5. Letter from Charlotte Brontë to W. S. Williams.
6. Letter from Charlotte Brontë to Ellen Nussey.
7. Letter from Charlotte Brontë to Ellen Nussey.
8. Crayon drawing of Charlotte Brontë and the portrait of the Duke of Wellington in Haworth Parsonage Museum.
9. Letter from Charlotte Brontë to W. S. Williams.

TWENTY-ONE

Conscience

Elizabeth Gaskell was at that time just forty years old—six years older than Charlotte. She was already a promising writer, having created something of a stir with her first novel, *Mary Barton*, which had been published in 1848. Mrs Gaskell, happily married with a family, had expressed a keen desire to meet the author of *Jane Eyre* and was frankly curious to learn details of a life so different from her own. What she could not learn from Charlotte, she gleaned—not always accurately—from her hostess.

Mrs Gaskell's first impression of Charlotte Brontë was conveyed by her in a letter to a friend.

She is (as she calls herself) *undeveloped*, thin, and more than half a head shorter than I am; soft brown hair, not very dark; eyes (very good and expressive, looking straight and open at you) of the same colour as her hair; a large mouth; the forehead square, broad, and rather overhanging. She has a very sweet voice; rather hesitates in choosing her expressions, but when chosen they seem without an effort admirable, and just befitting the occasion; there is nothing overstrained, but perfectly simple.[1]

Charlotte Brontë's own impression of Mrs Gaskell has not been preserved, but that the two ladies liked each other is evident for they were soon exchanging letters of friendship. They began by discussing various literary matters, but Charlotte still distrusted her own ability to inspire friendship, and wrote earnestly:

> I shall be glad to hear from you whenever you have time to write to me, but you are never, on any account, to do this except when inclination prompts and leisure permits. I should never thank you for a letter which you had felt it a task to write.[2]

Throughout the autumn of 1850, Charlotte was engaged upon a task which revived her most painful memories. Messrs Smith and Elder planned to re-issue *Wuthering Heights* and *Agnes Grey*, and she undertook to edit the works and write a preface to them.

To read again what her sisters had written was almost unbearable. She worked during the day because to read the books at night disturbed her dreams. It may have been during this time that she destroyed Emily's second novel, if, in fact, such a novel existed.

Of the theme of such a work nothing is known, but it is possible to hazard a guess. Charlotte knew that *Wuthering Heights* had given many people an unfavourable impression of her sister. She would have been eager to erase this impression. That she did not seems to suggest that a second book may have been on no pleasant subject.

Emily may have destroyed a book herself before her death, but if so why did she leave other unpublished writings?

From Charlotte's gross editing, we may infer that she destroyed indiscriminately too. However much we may quarrel with her well-meaning vandalism, nobody could find fault with the Biographical Notice of her sisters which prefaced the new edition of their novels. Emily and Anne not only produced works of genius, but were themselves the sources of inspiration. Branwell never painted more sensitively than when he depicted his sisters and Charlotte never wrote more incomparably than when she presented Emily and Anne to the world.

Of Emily's death, Charlotte declared:

> My sister, Emily, first declined. The details of her illness are deep-branded in my memory, but to dwell on them, either in thought or narrative, is not within my power. Never in all her life had she lingered over any task that lay before her, and she did not linger now. She sank rapidly. She made haste to leave us.

Yet, while physically she perished, mentally she grew stronger than we had yet known her. Day by day when I saw with what a front she met suffering, I looked on her with an anguish of wonder and love. I have seen nothing like it; but, indeed, I have never seen her parallel in anything. Stronger than a man, simpler than a child, her nature stood alone. The awful point was, that while full of truth for others, on herself she had no pity; the spirit was inexorable to the flesh; from the trembling hand, the unnerved limbs, the faded eyes, the same service was exacted as they had rendered in health. To stand by and witness this, and not dare to remonstrate, was a pain no words can render.

Of Anne's poems, Charlotte maintained,

To me, they seem sad, as if her whole innocent life had been passed under the martyrdom of an unconfessed physical pain; their effect, indeed, would be too distressing, were it not combated by the certain knowledge that in her last moments this tyranny of a too tender conscience was overcome; this pomp of terrors broke up, and passing away, left her dying hour unclouded. Her belief in God did not then bring to her dread, as of a stern Judge—but hope, as in a Creator and Saviour; and no faltering hope was it, but a sure and steadfast conviction, on which, in the rude passage from Time to Eternity, he threw the weight of her human weakness, and by which he was enabled to bear what was to be borne, patiently—serenely—victoriously.[3]

Privately, Charlotte wrote:

Her quiet, Christian death did not rend my heart as Emily's stern, simple, undemonstrative end did. I let Anne go to God and felt He had a right to her. I could hardly let Emily go. I wanted to hold her back then, and I want her back now. Anne, from her childhood, seemed preparing for an early death. Emily's spirit seemed strong enough to bear her to fulness of years.[4]

In the conclusion to her Biographical Notice, Charlotte wrote that she had deemed it a sacred duty to wipe the dust from their gravestones and leave their names free from soil. She evidently intended the confusion over the authorship of the books to be thus resolved. Her statement did not prevent later biographers from declaring that all the novels and poems had been written by Charlotte and that, of these, some had been dictated to Emily and Anne and signed by them.[5]

It does indeed seem odd that the poems she 'dictated' to Emily should be infinitely superior to the poems written in her own hand. Neither is it feasible to declare that the general untidiness and spelling errors of Emily's and Anne's manuscripts prove they were incapable of producing such poems. The ability to spell is not a criterion of genius. The inspiration which produced their work was not even constant. They wrote "when they were in the humour" and this was not every day. The gulf between their published work and the few private manuscripts that have survived points not to Charlotte's having been the sole writer in the family, but to their having written such poems and stories while under the influence of their creative faculties.

With her painful task complete, Charlotte sought release from her intolerable loneliness by accepting an invitation from Harriet Martineau to visit Ambleside.

Charlotte greatly enjoyed herself, writing,

> her visitors enjoy the most perfect liberty; what she claims for herself she allows them. I rise at my own hour, breakfast alone (she is up at five, takes a cold bath, and a walk by starlight, and has finished breakfast and got to her work by seven-o-clock) I pass the morning in the drawing-room—she in her study. At two-o-clock we meet, work, talk, walk together until five, her dinner-hour, spend the evening together, when she converses fluently and abundantly, and with the most complete frankness. I go to my own room soon after ten—she sits up writing till twelve.[6]

Perhaps it was during the long, quiet hours at Ambleside that Charlotte began to write *Villette*. The social engagements undertaken during this time were much to her liking. Together they visited Fox Howe, home of the late Matthew Arnold, where Charlotte met Arnold's son but was unfavourably impressed by his foppish conceit.

At Charlotte's insistence, Miss Martineau also conducted an experiment in mesmerism. The value of hypnotism in the curing of certain nervous disorders were just being realized, and Harriet Martineau had undergone mesmeric treatment and learnt the art herself. She was reluctant to practise upon her guest but Charlotte insisted and the experiment was made. Curiously, Miss Martineau stopped as soon as Charlotte called out that she was under the influence. The experiment was not to be resumed, despite Charlotte's pleas, because she considered it bad for her guest's nerves.

Miss Martineau, who related the event to Mrs Gaskell, was somewhat appalled at the ease with which Charlotte fell into a trance, and although admitting that she had made an excellent subject, was intelligent enough to perceive that great harm might result if Miss Brontë's repressed emotions were allowed to bubble to the surface of her consciousness.

Charlotte was indeed repressed, both socially and sexually. Yet she retained her belief that there can be no marriage without love; that it is better to remain a spinster than to wed for the sake of donning a wedding ring. Nevertheless, when a suitor loomed upon the horizon, Charlotte was sorely tempted. The gentleman in question was James Taylor, a partner in the firm of Messrs Smith and Elder, for whom Charlotte felt respect and liking, but no physical attraction.

Mr Taylor pressed his suit with some diligence, even visiting Charlotte at Haworth, where he performed the difficult feat of getting Mr Brontë to like him. Although she was aware that her father disliked the notion of her marrying, she was tempted by thoughts of security and escape from solitude but, when Mr Taylor confronted her in the Parsonage, she refused him.

> Now that he is away I feel more gently towards him; it is only close by that I grow rigid, stiffening with a strange mixture of apprehension and anger, which nothing softens but his retreat and a perfect subduing of his nature.[7]

Mr Taylor continued to enjoy the friendship of the woman he had wished to marry and his very kindness moved Charlotte to fresh regret at having turned down his offer. At thirty-five years of age a plain woman cannot afford to pick and choose and, seen in retrospect, Mr Taylor's diminutive stature, ginger hair and "determined, dreadful nose" were less repellant than before.

Charlotte passed a dreary winter, longing to leave home again, but uncomfortably aware that her new book was coming along very slowly.

> Besides I don't deserve to go to London; nobody merits a change or a treat less. I secretly think, on the contrary, I ought

to be put in prison, and kept on bread and water in solitary confinement—without even a letter from Cornhill—till I had written a book. One or two things would certainly result from such a mode of treatment pursued for twelve months; either I should come out at the end of that time with a three-volumed M.S. in my hand, or else with a condition of intellect that would exempt me ever after from literary efforts and expectations.[8]

Charlotte was greatly disturbed by reading Harriet Martineau's *Letters On The Nature And Development Of Man*. It was the first atheistical and materialistic treatise she had ever read and she was torn between the horror of the doctrine of spiritual annihilation and her anger against those critics who heaped scorn upon a woman she knew to be sincere.

Charlotte persuaded Ellen to spend some weeks with her during the early spring of 1851. After Ellen's departure, she had intended to settle seriously to her writing but loneliness drove her down to London. She made a trip to Leeds first in order to replenish her wardrobe, and bought a black silk dress, a white lace shawl and a bonnet lined with pink.

In London Charlotte stayed, as usual, with the Smiths and spent a month of intensive visiting. Apart from the ever-recurring migraine which caused her to complain, "I hoped to leave my headaches behind me at Haworth; but it seems I brought them carefully packed in my trunk, and very much have they been in my way since I came," she had to endure the scrutiny of complete strangers to whom she was pointed out as the famous Currer Bell.

Charlotte attended a series of lectures given by Thackeray and while enjoying the occasion, was horrified when the rest of the audience formed itself into two lines, down which she was forced to pass in order to reach the exit.·

The Great Exhibition at the Crystal Palace was visited five times. Charlotte considered it to be a noisy, overrated place but, at her father's request, she dutifully examined all the railway exhibits that she might describe them to him upon her return.

Charlotte also visited an exhibition of paintings at Somerset House, attended a Confirmation by Cardinal Wiseman in the Spanish Ambassador's Chapel, followed by an evening at a Quaker meeting. Samuel Rogers, the poet, she breakfasted with,

and went to the theatre to see a performance of the great
tragedienne, Rachel, which she described as

terrible, as if the earth had cracked deep at your feet, and
revealed a glimpse of hell. I shall never forget it. She made me
shudder to the marrow of my bones; in her some fiend has certainly taken up an incarnate home.

Two other visits were also of great interest. One was made,
under an assumed name, to a phrenologist who informed
Charlotte she was pessimistic and self-distrusting, passionate,
and capable of great achievements. She went, also, to hear
D'Aubigne, the French Protestant preacher, and wrote to Ellen:
"It was pleasant—half sweet, half sad—and strangely sug-
gestive, to hear the French language once more."

Charlotte broke her homeward journey at Manchester and
spent two days in the Gaskell home where she found her
hostess to be "a woman of many fine qualities and deserves the
epithet which I find is generally applied to her—charming".

Charlotte was, also, rather to her own surprise, charmed by
Mrs Gaskell's four little girls. The youngest of these, Julia, took
an inexplicable fancy to Miss Brontë and insisted upon holding
her hand. Charlotte was touched and flattered, but when Mrs
Gaskell told Julia to show the guest to some part of the house,
Charlotte cried, earnestly, "Oh, pray do not bid her do anything for me. It has been so sweet hitherto to have her rendering
her little kindnesses *spontaneously*."

Upon her return to Haworth, Charlotte wrote, playfully:

Could you manage to convey a small kiss to that dear, but dangerous little person, Julia? She surreptitiously possessed herself
of a minute fraction of my heart, which has been missing ever
since I saw her.

Haworth was still as desolate as ever. Charlotte settled to her
writing, recreating her Brussels experience, reliving the tormented emotions, stifled by her own conscience, and withered
by Heger's neglect.

The writing of *Villette* was a catharsis, but the strain told
on her health. Miserably, Charlotte wrote:

Such long, stormy days and nights there were, when I felt such
a craving for support and companionship as I cannot express.
Sleepless, I lay awake night after night, weak and unable to

occupy myself. I sat in my chair day after day, the saddest memories my only company.

When Mrs Gaskell urged a second visit, Charlotte declined, believing that it was weakness to ameliorate her lot.

The sudden death of Keeper, Emily's dog, did not help to brighten Charlotte's spirits. In desperation she appealed to Ellen to pay her a visit, but while her friend's company cheered her, the physical symptoms of nausea, insomnia and migraine continued.

Mr Brontë insisted that a doctor should be consulted and Charlotte's illness was diagnosed as "derangement of the liver".

The ever-present fear of consumption which hung over Charlotte was temporarily removed and she went, at the beginning of 1852, for a period of convalescence to the Nussey family. In this household, she could relax completely and be not Currer Bell, the famous writer, but Charlotte Brontë whom Ellen had befriended more than twenty years before.

Charlotte's publishers were pressing her for the new book, but she found it impossible to complete within any specified period. Apart from her uncertain state of health, which often caused her to lay her writing aside, she could work only when the mood was upon her. Sometimes, months would elapse before she could add anything to her story. Then she would see the next part so clearly in her mind that she had only to clothe the imagined incident in words. These she chose with the utmost care, writing on tiny scraps of paper held close to her eyes, then copied the finished paragraph into her manuscript.

At the end of June, Charlotte went, alone, to Scarborough to discover if her instructions regarding Anne's tombstone had been fulfilled. There were several mistakes in the lettering which needed rectification and having attended to these she remained for nearly a month before returning home.

Once again, loneliness, depression and physical indisposition incapacitated Charlotte. Mr Brontë and Tabby were both ailing and much of her time was occupied in nursing. Ellen came again to stay, but Charlotte allowed her to remain for only a week. The company of her oldest friend gave her the necessary solace which enabled her to bear her solitary existence and complete the novel.[9]

Charlotte had often complained because nobody was left with whom to discuss her writing. Mr Brontë, perhaps sensing this, begged her to read it aloud to him, and as she reached the concluding chapters asked, rather pathetically, that the story be given a happy ending. What her father could not realize was, that his daughter was psychologically incapable of providing one.

In *Villette* Charlotte had portrayed herself in the character of Lucy Snowe, the morbid, introspective school teacher who loves the fiery little Belgian, Paul Emmanuel. To allow them to marry would have been to set the tacit seal of approval upon her passion for Monsieur Heger. This her conscience would not allow her to do.

To please Mr Brontë she veiled Paul Emmanuel's death by drowning in a passage of rhetoric which deceived the more insensitive reader. Charlotte could not deceive herself. The flame of love for Heger was finally quenched in the waters of the Channel which separated Lucy Snowe from Paul Emmanuel.

NOTES TO CHAPTER TWENTY-ONE

1. Most of the facts in this chapter have been culled from Mrs Gaskell's *Life of Charlotte Brontë*.
2. Letter from Charlotte Brontë to Mrs Gaskell, 27th August 1850.
3. Charlotte Brontë, Biographical Notice of Ellis and Acton Bell.
4. Charlotte Brontë, Memoir of Anne Brontë.
5. John Malham-Dembleby, *The Confessions of Charlotte Brontë*.
6. Letter from Charlotte Brontë to Ellen Nussey.
7. Letter from Charlotte Brontë to Ellen Nussey.
8. Letter from Charlotte Brontë to W. S. Williams.
9. Mrs Gaskell, *Life of Charlotte Brontë*.

TWENTY-TWO

My Dear Arthur

Life has a habit of offering gifts when we least expect or want them. The writing of *Villette* had scarcely purged Charlotte of the residue of her Belgian emotions, when another love was offered. It came from her father's curate who asked for her hand in marriage—not decorously in the restrained etiquette of the time, but passionately and stirringly.

He spoke of sufferings he had borne for months, of sufferings he could endure no longer, and craved leave for some hope. I could only entreat him to leave me then and promise a reply on the morrow. I asked him if he had spoken to Papa. He said, he dared not. I think I half-led, half put him out of the room. When he was gone I immediately went to Papa and told him what had taken place.[1]

Mr Brontë's reaction was a violent fit of rage which frightened Charlotte and has disgusted biographers ever since. Selfish and intolerant the old man undoubtedly was, but few have cared to look at the situation through his eyes. His one surviving child was a delicate woman, already past the age at which it was considered safe to bear a first child. She was also famous and the only one to achieve any degree of worldly success.

Mr Brontë considered it dangerous for Charlotte to contemplate matrimony at all. He considered it unspeakable that she should ever think of accepting a penniless curate.

Human nature is unpredictable. During the scandals of

Branwell's later years, not a door in Haworth had been closed to him. When Arthur Bell Nicholls, conscientious, loyal and high-principled, made a perfectly respectable offer of marriage to Miss Brontë, he was scorned by all. John Brown even went so far as to declare publicly that he deserved to be shot. Charlotte, always on the side of the weaker battalions, was indignant at such injustice and greatly relieved when Mr Nicholls resigned his curacy and announced his intentions of doing missionary work in Australia.

Gladly did Charlotte accept an invitation to visit the Smiths again, in order to await the publication of *Villette*, which had been delayed in order not to conflict with the publication of Mrs Gaskell's new novel, *Ruth*.

Upon this occasion, Charlotte firmly insisted upon going where *she* wished to go. She was shown around Newgate Prison, the Bank, the Exchange, the Foundling Hospital and Bethlehem, where lunatics were then confined. Her choice of sightseeing was so extraordinary that one cannot help wondering if she were gathering possible material for a novel.

Villette was published on 24th January 1853 and was met immediately by lavish praise from every critic except Harriet Martineau.

Miss Martineau heartily detested the strong sexual feelings which run like electric currents through the narrative. She considered it coarse and unnatural for the female characters in the tale to be so hungry for love. She considered quite sincerely that the description of such feelings cheapened the book.

Charlotte, never one to take criticism lightly, was bitterly hurt at the accusation of coarseness. What Miss Martineau could not be expected to realize was, that in condemning the ardent nature of Lucy Snowe, she was, in fact, condemning Charlotte herself.

Charlotte immediately ended her friendship with Miss Martineau—an estrangement that remained permanent.

Back at Haworth, preparations were under way for a forthcoming social event. The Bishop of Ripon had condescended to visit the parish and would naturally expect to be entertained. The Parsonage was in a pleasant bustle, marred only by Mr Nicholls, on the eve of his formal resignation, who hovered

M

gloomily about the front hall and stared so hard at Charlotte that she was driven to the refuge of her bedroom.

The Bishop came and proved to be "the most benignant little gentleman that ever put on lawn sleeves". He was also a very understanding gentleman who, having ascertained the cause of Mr Nicholls' obvious dejection, singled him out for a kind word.

Mr Nicholls was, indeed, beginning to have second thoughts about going to Australia. Hoping, perhaps, that the Bishop might have spoken on his behalf, he asked Mr Brontë for permission to withdraw his resignation. Permission was granted, on condition that he agreed never to mention again the subject of marriage. Mr Nicholls indignantly refused, infuriating Mr Brontë but earning Charlotte's respect for his constancy.

It was a relief to go visiting once more—to Manchester, where Mrs Gaskell, to whom Charlotte had confided something of the state of affairs, welcomed her kindly. Upon her return, Mrs Gaskell evidently sent Charlotte a copy of Thackeray's *Lecture on Fielding*, in which the former had joked about the vices of the latter.

Charlotte felt such an attitude keenly.

> I believe, if only once the prospect of a promising life blasted on the outset by wild ways had passed close under his eyes, he never *could* have spoken with such levity of what led to its piteous destruction.[2]

Charlotte returned home in time to bid Mr Nicholls goodbye. His departure was spectacular. At the final communion service, when called upon to administer the sacrament to Charlotte, he broke down and could barely complete the service.

Charlotte, hideously embarrassed, was also touched and flattered. Mr Brontë evidently believed that Haworth had seen the back of this most troublesome curate, for Mr Nicholls' new post was near Pontefract. He was blissfully unaware of the fact that his dutiful daughter was corresponding with Mr Nicholls.

Mr Nicholls evidently wrote first and Charlotte replied, with increasing sympathy, remembering, perhaps, the letters she had once written with as great a need.

At the end of September, Mrs Gaskell visited Haworth for the first time, and wrote her account of a life so different from any she had ever imagined.

No one comes to the house; nothing disturbs the deep repose; hardly a voice is heard; you catch the ticking of the clock in the kitchen, or the buzzing of a fly in the parlour, all over the house. Miss Brontë sits alone in her parlour; breakfasting with her father in his study at nine-o-clock. She helps in the housework, for one of their servants, Tabby, is nearly ninety, and the other only a girl. Then I accompanied her in her walks on the sweeping moors; the heather-bloom had been blighted by a thunder-storm a day or two before, and was all of a livid brown colour, instead of a blaze of purple glory it ought to have been. Oh! those high, wild, desolate moors up above the whole world, and the very realms of silence! Home to dinner at two. Mr Brontë has his dinner sent in to him. All the small table arrangements had the same dainty simplicity about them. Then we rested, and talked over the clear, bright fire—I soon observed that her habits for order were such that she could not go on with the conversation if a chair was out of its place; everything was arranged with delicate regularity—We have generally had another walk before tea, which is at six; at half-past eight, prayers; and by nine all the household are in bed, except ourselves. We sit up together till ten or past; and after I go I hear Miss Brontë come down and walk up and down the room for an hour or so.

Charlotte talked constantly of her sisters, a subject that she and her father might have avoided, each hoping not to re-open an old wound. Mrs Gaskell was keenly interested, but somewhat repelled by what she learnt of Emily's character. Her intensely feminine nature shrank from one whom she pictured as "a remnant of the Titans—great-grand-daughter of the giants who used to inhabit the earth".[3]

It is not known if Charlotte asked Mrs Gaskell for advice concerning her relationship with Mr Nicholls. She evidently took Ellen into her confidence and was equally obviously told to put all thoughts of marriage out of her mind. Ellen did not relish the idea of her friend marrying and told her so. That Charlotte was beginning to feel a certain affection for the long-suffering curate is demonstrated by the sudden cessation of warmth in her letters to Ellen Nussey. No longer did she write, as she had in the Spring of 1836, "If you love me, *do, do, do,* come on Friday; I shall watch and wait for you, and if you disappoint me I shall weep."[4]

Throughout the winter, her notes to Ellen ended formally, "yours faithfully, C. Brontë".

Charlotte no longer relied exclusively upon Ellen for affection. She had widened her circle of acquaintances, and was being drawn into a close liaison with Mr Nicholls.

It is fashionable to imagine that Charlotte finally accepted Arthur Bell Nicholls out of pity. This seems most unlikely. True, there are in her letters none of the brilliant hopes of youth, not even an echo of passion; but Charlotte was two years short of forty, crushed by tragedy and determined never to anticipate pleasure lest she be called upon to endure disappointment.

Yet some feeling warmer than pity, stronger even than her dread of solitude, must have overwhelmed her sense of duty and her conventional code of morality. Something stronger than respect must have sent her to the neighbouring village of Oxenhope, where she and Mr Nicholls could meet in secret and discuss the position.

In April 1854, Mr Brontë finally consented to an engagement; it was a defeat of the Irish by the Irish, but Mr Brontë did not surrender unconditionally. Mr Nicholls could marry Charlotte on condition that they lived at the Parsonage and did not alter any of the household arrangements or attempt to share Mr Brontë's study. The conditions were agreed and the spoils of war wrote demurely:

> I trust to love my husband—I am grateful for his tender love to me. I believe him to be an affectionate, a conscientious, a high-principled man; and if, with all this, I should yield to regrets, that fine talents, congenial tastes, and thoughts are not added, it seems to me I should be most presumptuous and thankless.[5]

The marriage was to take place at the end of June, and Charlotte's time was fully occupied with extensive preparations. She converted the little room behind the parlour into a study for her husband.

> Since I came home I have been very busy stitching; the little new room is got into order, and the green and white curtains are up; they exactly suit the papering and look neat and clean enough.

Ellen, with whom the quarrel had been resolved, and Miss Wooler, were the only guests bidden to the ceremony. Both ladies arrived the day before and were present when Mr Brontë, with a last gesture of defiant selfishness, announced he had no intention of going to the service.

There was consternation, until Miss Wooler offered to give the bride away—the sex of this personage not being particularized in Holy Writ.

Mr Nicholls had fully acceded to Charlotte's request for a quiet wedding. He was, after all, in love with Miss Brontë, the parson's daughter. For Currer Bell, he cared little. Nevertheless, several villagers were standing about to watch her take the short walk to the church. There, a few feet away from her dead brother and sisters, she stood in a white dress and bonnet trimmed with green leaves in order to become Mrs Nicholls.

The honeymoon consisted of a trip to Ireland, during which Charlotte fell deeply in love with her new husband. The portrait of black-whiskered Arthur Bell Nicholls shows an unrelenting profile to the world.* To his wife he displayed not only his own passion, but also re-awakened her own.

Charlotte's letters brim over with happiness she can scarcely confine within the boundary of the printed word.

I really seem to have had scarcely a spare moment since that dim quiet June morning, when you, Ellen and myself all walked down to Haworth Church. Not that I have been wearied or oppressed; but the fact is, my time is not my own now; somebody else wants a good portion of it, and says, "We must do so and so." We *do* so and so accordingly; and it generally seems the right thing.[6]

Mr Nicholls was proving to be a loving and possessive husband. He liked his wife to help him in his parish duties, to sit and talk with him in the evening and to devote her leisure to his comfort as he devoted his leisure to hers.

Mr Nicholls disapproved of the letters that passed between Charlotte and Ellen, probably because he considered their affection too marked, their expressions too unconventional. He insisted that Ellen promise to burn Charlotte's letters as soon as she had read them, else he would elect himself as censor. Ellen gave her word and, to the immeasurable relief of all

* Portrait is now in Haworth Parsonage Museum.

subsequent biographers, conveniently forgot to keep her promise.

Charlotte, for so long virtually her own mistress, thought her husband's strictures highly amusing and was not in the least annoyed by them. For her he was now "my dear Arthur" or "my dear boy" and not the least cause of her gratitude was the unexpected harmony between Mr Nicholls and Mr Brontë, who apparently agreed that their truce was to remain unbroken.

The only event that saddened Charlotte was the death of Flossy, the old spaniel which had belonged to Anne. But this sorrow was mitigated for Charlotte by the comforting reflection that "no dog ever had a happier life or easier death".

Shortly before Christmas, Mr Nicholls persuaded his wife to take a walk over the moors to the waterfall, as he thought, that after a recent snowfall, the sight would give her pleasure. They undertook the four-mile walk in high spirits and arrived home drenched to the skin, in consequence of a sudden storm.

The chill with which Charlotte woke on the following morning was not severe enough to warrant anxiety. She went with her husband, early in the New Year, to visit the Kay-Shuttle-worths, but returned with a sore throat, having unwisely gone for a walk on snow-covered ground.

The cold increased and lingered, complicated by nausea and faintness. She had begun a new novel, *Emma*, but the work was laid aside, and a doctor called in. The doctor informed Charlotte that she was pregnant—news which should have cheered and relieved her—but the nausea and faintness continued unabated.

In February, Tabby died suddenly and the event, although it had been expected for some time, deeply depressed Charlotte, who found no pleasure even in talking of the coming baby.

To Martha, who helped to nurse her mistress, she said, "I am sure that I will love it when it comes, but I am so tired."

Eventually, Charlotte was forced to go to bed from where she wrote, in faint, barely legible pencil-marks:

> I am not going to talk of my sufferings—it would be useless and painful. I want to give you an assurance, which I know will comfort you—and that is, that I find in my husband the tenderest nurse, the kindest support, the best earthly comfort that woman ever had. His patience never fails and it is tried by sad days and broken nights.[7]

Martha complained that Charlotte ate scarcely enough to keep a thrush alive, and her constant nausea was distressing to witness.

Spring came, and with it an upsurge of hope, as she asked eagerly for food. It was only a temporary respite. Consumption, the old enemy of the house, had been awakened into life by the susceptibility of an early pregnancy.

Charlotte roused briefly in order to whisper to her husband, "I am not going to die, am I? He will not separate us; we have been so happy."

A day or two later, the lych-gate was opened again, and Charlotte Brontë passed into the shade of the old church for the last time. Behind her, in the garden, the two fir trees, planted on her wedding morning, were beginning to thrive.

Old Mr Brontë, who had attended the death bed unflinchingly, had made arrangements for the funeral in a crisply efficient manner that somewhat shocked the villagers. Only Martha, coming into his room with clean linen, heard him sobbing, "Oh, my poor little Charlotte! My dear little girl!"

The servant laid the clean linen on the bed and silently withdrew. Her tasks were not yet finished, nor could the death of this last child mitigate her responsibilities to the family. For the six years that followed she would serve Mr Brontë faithfully until he too was carried through the lych-gate. After that the Parsonage held no longer those whom she had loved, and when Mr Nicholls returned to Ireland to marry his cousin, another Charlotte, Martha went too. It is less lonely to talk with those who remember than to read in cold words cut into harsh stone the names of those who cannot return.

NOTES TO CHAPTER TWENTY-TWO

1. Letter from Charlotte Brontë to Ellen Nussey.
2. Letter from Charlotte Brontë to Mrs Gaskell.
3. Mrs Gaskell, *Life of Charlotte Brontë*.
4. Letter from Charlotte Brontë to Ellen Nussey.
5. Letter from Charlotte Brontë to Ellen Nussey.
6. Letter from Charlotte Brontë to Miss Wooler.
7. Letter from Charlotte Brontë to Ellen Nussey.

Postscript

Those who visit Haworth today must leave their cars at the top of the hill and proceed on foot, if they wish to derive the greatest pleasure from their stay.

The main street is still cobbled, as it was on that cold February day in 1820, when the Rev. Patrick Brontë brought his family to their new home.

That home is now a Museum, built upon by Mr Brontë's successor, its garden neatly tended, its rooms kept at a carefully warm temperature. On the walls hang neat little printed notices, giving the visitor pertinent information. The rooms are partly furnished, the sitting-room and study appearing today as they did in Charlotte's time. Tourists move quietly through the house, as if by unspoken consent unwilling to disturb the privacy of the family. The atmosphere is almost reverent, as if the tourist were an intruder and might be confronted by Mr Brontë, politely enquiring the nature of his business.

From the windows one may look out upon the grey tombstones where the Binns, Hatterslays and Browns of previous generations sleep undisturbed.

At the 'Black Bull', situated closer to the Parsonage than one might imagine from description, the inhabitants of Haworth still gather to drink their pint of ale, and answer questions with the blunt good-humour of a native Yorkshireman. A porch has been added to the building now, and the bar within, instead of occupying half the area of the saloon, has been pushed back into a discreet recess. But the lights are dim, and it requires only the slightest effort of the imagination to see the slight, red-haired figure stumble in, lift his tall hat in greeting to the land-lady, and wander down the little corridor to the room on the left, where a pull at a rope would bring the relief of gin.

Behind the Parsonage stretch the steep, bleak fields, crowned with stone. I set out early in the morning to explore them— a cold blustery day with mud deep in the lane. Out of the gates which led to the unforgivably neglected school-house, where the Brontës once held Sunday-school classes, ran a very small, very grubby boy. So much a part of the strange atmosphere did he seem that it would not have surprised me to hear him say, "Heathcliff and Cathy are up yonder, and I darnut pass 'em."

But this was a son of the twentieth century so used to the whims of tourists that, unbidden, he volunteered the informa-tion that to reach the Brontë waterfall, I must "pass t'beck and goa thro' t'fields"—then scampered away.

I wondered, briefly, if the shadows of six tiny children ever accompanied him, if their treble voices might even yet be heard above the screeching of the wind and the mud be imprinted, for an instant of time, with the impression of feet.

But when I looked back the lane was empty.

General Bibliography

The Life of Charlotte Brontë by Elizabeth G. Gaskell. (Oxford University Press)
The Brontë Story by Margaret Lane. (William Heinemann Ltd)
The Confessions of Charlotte Brontë by John Malham-Dembleby. (Published privately by Mrs Leah Malham-Dembleby)
The Infernal World of Branwell Brontë by Daphne du Maurier. (Gollancz Ltd)
Anne Brontë—Her Life and Work by Ada Harrison and Derek Stanford. (Methuen Ltd)
Branwell Brontë by Winifred Gerin. (Nelson and Sons Ltd)
Anne Brontë by Winifred Gerin. (Nelson and Sons Ltd)
Gondal's Queen by Emily Jane Brontë, edited and arranged by F. E. Ratchford. (Nelson, Texas)
The Brontë's Web of Childhood by F. E. Ratchford. (University of Columbia Press)
The Brontës—Charlotte and Emily by Laura L. Hinkley. (Hammond, Hammond and Company Ltd)
The Complete Poems of Emily Brontë, edited and introduced by Philip Henderson. (The Folio Society)
Biographical Introduction to *The Professor* by Phyllis Bentley. (Collins)

Index

INDEX

Brönte, Charlotte—*cont.*

James; as governess, 42–3, 72–3; early writings, 43; first train journey, 44; love of sketching, 44–5; *quoted* on Emily, 54, 61, 127–8, 168–9; *quoted* on Anne, 62, 169; paints portrait of William Weightman, 69; abortive school project, 73, 90–1; in Belgium, 76, 78–80, 84, 86–9; poems *quoted*, 90; *quoted* on E. and A. Bell, 106, 127–8; washes hands of Branwell during Thorp Green scandal, 112–13; accompanies father to Manchester for eye operation, 115–16; growing success, 129–30; on "tricky" advertising, 135; in London, 136–7; 161–2, 165, 172–3; 177; at Branwell's death, 145–6; cares for Anne after Emily's death, 151–3; with Anne at her death in Scarborough, 154–7; loneliness after Anne's death, 159–60, 163, 173–5; Harriet Martineau and, 161–2, 170–1, 172, 177; first meeting with Mrs Gaskell, 165, 167–8; Mrs Gaskell's description of, 167; proposed to by James Taylor, 171; engagement and marriage to Mr Nicholls, 176–82; death, 183. *For publications see under specific titles*
——, Elizabeth, 12, 14, 18, 20, 23, 32, 80
——, Emily Jane, birth and early years, 12–15; childhood, 18, 22–8; home education, 22–3; the "infernal world", 23–8, 104, *see also* "Angria", "Gondal"; "diary paper" (1834), *quoted*, 33; Branwell's portrait of, 35; as teacher in Halifax, 39, 58; at Roe Head, 54; poems *quoted*, 55, 56, 57,

58, 59, 74, 75, 84–5, 104; homesickness, 55; character and talents, 55–7; divided personality, 56–61, 74–5; suggested Lesbianism of, 60; friendship with William Weightman, 69; in Brussels, 78–83; as housekeeper at Haworth, 84; "diary paper" (1845) *quoted*, 102–3; reluctance to publish poems, 106–7; physical strength and self-possession of, 113–14; Charlotte on genius of, 127–8; increasing ill-health, 145, 146–7; attitude to death, 146–7; death, 147–9; Charlotte on death of, 168–9. *For publications see under specific titles*
——, Maria (née Branwell), 11–15, 141
——, Maria, 12, 14, 16–20, 23, 32, 80
——, Rev. Patrick, early life, 9–11; physical appearance, 11; marriage, 11–12; attempts at writing, 11; appointed to Haworth, 12–14; abnormal dread of fire, 14–15; declares Maria to be his cleverest child, 16; gives children home education, 22–3; encourages them to keep pets, 23; shocked at Charlotte's and Ellen's proposed seaside holiday, 44; remedy for intoxication, 49; recalls Branwell from Bradford, 50; notes on Branwell's health, 51; affection for William Weightman, 68; doubtful about private school project, 73; escorts Charlotte and Emily to Brussels, 78; visits Thorp Green, 94; moves into Branwell's bedroom during Thorp Green scandal, 112; failing sight, and operation, 115–16, 158; reaction to suc-

Elkr

Deborah Chaplin